FILLED TO OVERFLOWING

CAROLE MAYHALL

faith

NAVPRESS ⬤®
A MINISTRY OF THE NAVIGATORS
P.O. Box 6000, Colorado Springs, Colorado 80934

The Navigators is an international Christian
organization. Jesus Christ gave His followers the
Great Commission to go and make disciples
(Matthew 28:19). The aim of The Navigators
is to help fulfill that commission by multiplying
laborers for Christ in every nation.

NavPress is the publishing ministry of The
Navigators. NavPress publications are tools to
help Christians grow. Although publications alone
cannot make disciples or change lives, they can
help believers learn biblical discipleship and
apply what they learn to their lives and ministries.

© 1984 by Carole Mayhall
All rights reserved, including translation
Library of Congress Catalog Card
Number: 84-060517
ISBN: 0-89109-517-9
15172

Third printing, 1986

Unless otherwise identified, Scripture quotations
are from the *Holy Bible: New International Version*
(NIV). Copyright © 1973, 1978, 1984, International
Bible Society. Used by permission of Zondervan
Bible Publishers. Other versions used include the
King James Version (KJV); *The New Testament
in Modern English, Revised Edition* by J.B. Phillips
(*Phillips*), © 1958, 1960, 1972 by J.B. Phillips,
published by The Macmillan Company, New York;
The Living Bible, © 1971 by Tyndale House
Publishers; *The New American Standard Bible*
(NASB), © The Lockman Foundation 1960, 1962,
1963, 1968, 1971, 1972, 1973, 1975, 1977; and
The Amplified Bible (AMP), © 1965 by Zondervan
Publishing House.

Printed in the United States of America

Dear Father,

> You've just asked me
> > that question You
> > asked the blind man
> > on Your way to Jericho:

"What do you want Me to do for you?"

I answered,

> "Please raise up Jim.
> Please heal Joye.
> Please give Jack wisdom."

"No, that wasn't My question, child.
What do you want Me to do for *you*?"

I stopped to ponder.

> "Lord, I want to fully
> > experience
> > You."

He whispered softly,

"Good. I want
that, too."

To Eric
        and Sunny,
my grandchildren.
May you grow to be filled to overflowing
with all the glories of God's riches!

Contents

Author

Carole Mayhall is a popular Christian communicator. She has traveled throughout the world speaking to women at seminars and conferences on the subject of discipleship.

Carole is a graduate of Wheaton College with a degree in Christian Education. She and her husband, Jack, have served in the Navigator ministry for many years. Jack is the former U.S. Director of The Navigators. The Mayhalls live in Colorado Springs. Their daughter, Lynn, is married to Navigator staff member Tim Westberg.

Other NavPress books by Carole Mayhall:
> *Lord, Teach Me Wisdom*
> *From the Heart of a Woman*
> *Lord of My Rocking Boat*
> *Marriage Takes More Than Love*
>   (co-authored with Jack Mayhall)
> *Words that Hurt, Words that Heal:*
>   *Using Your Tongue as an Instrument of Blessing*

Introduction

All the balconies of the U-shaped hotel faced the Pacific Ocean, a slate-gray backdrop for the yachts and sailboats bobbing gently in the protected harbor. It was early—6:00 A.M.—and the sun was only beginning to touch the sky, sketching an outline of pink around the clouds, streaking the dawn with muted golds and soft pastels.

There on our tiny balcony I was taking a moment to thank and praise my Father for the blessings of our extensive ministry trip. As I glanced down several floors to my left, I was delighted to see one other woman on her porch. I thought, "She too must be up to see the wonders of the sunrise and to thank the Creator."

Then, startled, I blinked and looked again. This woman, up so early on this spectacular day, was playing solitaire!

The two of us seemed to be reflections of the two basic choices we are given in this life: God or solitaire. An absorption with the Creator or with the creature.

Both secular and religious sources are bombarding us with the solitaire message: Look out for number one, demand your rights, expect riches and prosperity, center your thinking on yourself.

But I don't see it working. I see very few happy people out there. Instead, I see the storm clouds of people demanding their rights, fulfilling their egos, and being absorbed by their own needs, raining all over their parade, preventing *true* contentment and fulfillment.

God has spelled out His answer to this dilemma. He tells us what we are to be filled with, what blocks this filling process, and how our fulfillment is accomplished.

This book is an attempt to get you to think, to study, to pray. I hope it will boggle your mind and challenge you to dig into the depths of God's riches, for therein you can search and find the reality of *true fulfillment.*

Whether you live in the dawn, morning, afternoon, or evening of your life, may you not be found playing spiritual solitaire. Rather, may you be found living a life filled *to overflowing* with God Himself.

1
Looking to Jesus

THE HAIR DRYER clicked off. Voices that had been blurred by the hum of the dryer now focused sharply. A ripple of laughter eddied around me.

I found myself unavoidably tuning in on a discussion about what should be done in case of a nuclear attack. Three women were agreeing that to try to flee the city before it was demolished would be futile. But what *should* they do?

Most people in Colorado Springs are aware that in the event of a nuclear attack, we would be leveled by the missiles aimed at Cheyenne Mountain. For beneath Cheyenne Mountain, which can be seen from anywhere in the city, are seven miles of tunnels housing the North American Air Defense Command—NORAD.

One woman said, "Well, I hope when it comes, I'll be in bed! I'd rather die in bed, especially if I'm in bed with someone I love." The others smiled and agreed that that would be a good idea.

Another woman, who had obviously had to diet all her life, contributed this gem: "Well, I'm going to keep a giant hot-fudge sundae in my freezer, and when the alarm sounds, I'm going to rush to the refrigerator and eat it—and everything else in sight."

Everyone laughed. But the laughter was bordered by fear. And I noticed that these women were not saying "*if* a nuclear attack comes" but "*when* it comes," as if the future menaced them with inevitable doom.

I wanted to come from under the dryer to give each lady a hug and say, "You know, there is Someone who holds the fate of the world in His hands. He promised us, 'Though the earth be removed and the mountains carried into the sea, I am in your midst.' His name is Jesus."

How often our focus is shown in casual conversation. Our thinking, our mindset, is disclosed by nearly everything we do and say. Our attitudes reveal our focus. The conversation of those women in the beauty shop indicated their fear, frustration, and anxiety.

What a contrast to the outlook of Elisabeth Elliot, who returned to the dangerous jungles of Ecuador to reach out to the tribe of Indians who had brutally murdered her husband and four other missionaries. Elisabeth and her four-year-old daughter, Valerie, went back to a section of jungle notorious for its poisonous snakes. Just imagine your four-year-old walking around barefoot in such a place! Yet Elisabeth wrote from that jungle, "God has delivered me from *all* fear."

Psalm 34:4 promises, "I sought the Lord, and He answered me, and delivered me from all my fears" (NASB). Elisabeth's focus on God enabled her to have a courageous, fearless attitude.

***

Our focus is revealed by our attitude about life in general. But I am finding mine is also exposed by attitudes and feelings I have about *me*.

In a message about self-worth, Ruth Myers pointed out that we are always looking into a mirror of some kind for our feelings of self-worth. Usually we peer into the mirror of other people's opinions about us. We are convinced that they are accepting or rejecting us (as indeed some of them are) because of our appearance, performance, or status. But these three factors are like a three-legged stool: If any one of them breaks down, our self-esteem takes a devastating tumble.

As I listened to Ruth, I thought to myself, "What events this week are going to demonstrate the basis of *my* self-worth?"

Later that week I was to speak to a group of women on the North Shore of Chicago. But for the first time in my life, I developed an infection in my eye. Getting up in front of those women with my eye swollen and half-closed made me feel *ugly*. As my feelings about myself took a nose-dive, I had to acknowledge I was looking into the mirror of people's opinions again—in this case, about my *appearance*.

A day or so before this occasion, I was driving around the North Shore in a borrowed car trying to find the home of a friend, the office of the eye doctor, and other places. I kept getting lost, and so I was late to each of my appointments. I chided, "Good grief, Carole. Can't you even find your way around a city where you lived for fourteen years?" I was depending on *performance* for a large part of my self-worth.

And *status*? Well, I have always been—and felt like it, too—very *average*. No one really wants to be average. But I was the middle child of a middle-class family living in a middle-sized town in middle America. I was never valedictorian or a drum majorette. Never abused by my family. Never been in jail. Just *average*. As a mother, I didn't even come up to average (which at the time was 2.2 children, I think). God gave us only one (but she's a humdinger).

I prayed, "Oh, Lord, I'm doing it *again*! I'm looking at how I think people perceive me. I'm focusing on myself, wondering how I look, how I perform, and what my status is. Instead I need to look into the mirror of Your love for me. I know that You love and accept me completely. Help me, Father, to always remember that!"

I find that whenever (and it happens often, I'm ashamed to tell you) I get my eyes off *who God is*, concentrating instead on *what I'm not*, I get discouraged.

***

Our focus is demonstrated by contentment—or lack of it—in who we are and what we are doing.

My attention was once caught by an article called "The Golden Years." The author begins:

> I've been thinking a lot lately about the so-called "Golden Years." Like most women, I had accepted a dictionary definition of the term as the "period in life after middle age, traditionally characterized by wisdom, contentment and useful leisure."
>
> I can't accept it now.
>
> "Wisdom" and "contentment" are only words, after all,

and words are only symbols, and symbols buy us very little at the supermarket. We need the cold hard ring of truth now and then—that truth which will work for us at the checkout counters of our own lives.

The author tells of interviewing four friends, spanning four basic age groups, and hearing these comments:

(age 31) "Golden Years? I have so much to do before then that I doubt I'll ever have them. I have to help my husband succeed. I want to raise our children decently—to get them ready for a very tough world. And of course, I want time for me, to find myself, to be my own person."

(age 44) "Only 20 years to go. I just hope we make it. If we can just get the kids through college and on their own. If we can keep my husband's blood pressure under control and see me sanely through menopause—that's what I mean about hoping we get there."

(age 53) "Sometimes I think our Golden Years will never come. My parents are still alive, and need constant attention. Our daughter was divorced last year, and lives with us again. Of course, she had a baby, and of course, my husband and I feel responsible—both for her and our grandson."

(age 63) "We're supposed to be on the brink, aren't we? Well, we're not. I'll be frank. We thought we were saving enough to live comfortably ever after, but we haven't —inflation has eaten it up. Now my husband talks about deferring his retirement. If he does, so will I—keeping a house much too big for us. We're both unhappy about the way things have turned out."

The author wanted to say, "Dear gals, don't you see that a whole Golden Year, or ten, may never come? Please don't wait, don't postpone. Live now, as wisely and contentedly as you can."

She went on to say, "Each of us must discover for herself that the grace and goodness of life do not depend on clock or calendar. That joy is not a time but a condition of the spirit. That any hour or day or week may be magic if we bring perception and appreciation to them.

"Let our hearts and senses be our dictionaries then. They will tell us, more personally than language, at least one truth we need to know. That waiting will not bring the Golden Years. But seeing and caring and living—not in the past, not in the future, but in the precious present—will."[1]

***

Our actions and words expose us, graphically revealing what we are thinking about. And most of the time in the marketplace of life, we display a "me first" philosophy.

From time to time Jack and I have the privilege of sharing a marriage seminar with various groups around the country. One of the points we emphasize is that husbands and wives need to know and feel that they are number one in the thoughts of their spouse—after God Himself.

At one seminar, a husband privately shared this interesting example with us. He and a friend had taken refuge from a storm under a small tree (they thought lightning hit only the big ones) when suddenly lightning struck, traveling down the trunk of the tree, knocking his friend unconscious, jumping to the metal trim in his belt, leaping around his waist, and temporarily paralyzing him from the waist down. As soon as possible, he telephoned his wife from the hospital. He said, "Don't worry, dear, but I was struck by lightning. I'm in the hospital now." His wife shouted, "Well, what am *I* supposed to do? The *car* won't start!"

He told this story with a wry smile that did not quite reach his eyes. The wife's first thought had been for herself—her own predicament.

A woman once told me of the death of her husband, and then added, "The thing I am having the most difficulty forgetting—forgiving, really—is the time I had to drive myself to the hospital for a hysterectomy because it was my husband's afternoon to play golf." The central concern in that husband's mind was his golf game.

We are being told these days that we have to look out for number one. Brazen voices tell us, "If I don't look out for me, nobody else will!" *My* happiness, *my* ego, and *my* satisfaction head the list of what is supposedly important.

***

But that's not what God says. He tells us to seek Him and His kingdom first. He says that even if we gain the whole world, if we don't have Him we don't have anything at all.

Like a constantly turning prism reflecting a multitude of colors, so my focus, my mindset, is manifested on the walls of my life in splintered and fractured hues. My attitude about myself and others reveals my focus; my priorities and contentment reflect this same focus.

The object of my attention, the focal point of my existence, is so vital, so important that I must listen carefully to God when He speaks to this issue. And He does speak. Clearly. He not only tells us where our focus is to be; He tells us how to get it and keep it there.

NOTES: 1. Kate Swarthout, "The Golden Years," *Frontier Magazine*, February 1981.

APPLICATION BIBLE STUDY

1. Read Psalm 62 and mark the places where the words "only" and "alone" are used relating to God. What needs are we to have met in God alone? List at least four.

2. The psalmist says he looks only to God for his security. What do you count on to provide you with security besides God? To provide hope? Deliverance? Rest?

3. List at least three of your inward fears.

4. Write out Psalm 34:4 in your own words. How does this verse apply to your list in question 3?

5. What steps are you taking to have your personal security and worth bound up in God alone?

2
Beholding Him

J ACK WAS GOING THROUGH an extremely painful time of stress
recently, and I was hurting because he was hurting. Yet
during the several weeks of trauma, the face of Christ was
superimposed over the problem. I could visualize Him standing over us, arms outstretched, saying, "This is from Me,
and it comes with love." As a result, even while aching
with Jack I was peaceful.

The following week another blow hit below the belt,
and suddenly the face of Christ slid off the screen of my
mind and I was left staring at an ugly, seemingly overwhelming problem. I cried for hours.

In my human state of imperfection, this will continue

to happen from time to time. But I want it to happen *less and less*. God asks...pleads...demands...commands that we set our minds "on things above, not on earthly things" (Colossians 3:2). More and more I want to be able to do just that. This truth is the most practical, stress-relieving, joy-fulfilling, peace-indwelling command God ever gave.

As I read those words from Colossians, I thought, "Yes, Lord, that is what I want to do. But the world keeps crowding in and pushing You out, and I keep letting it. I want to set my heart on You and on the treasures You have for me, but how do I *do* that?"

God said quietly to my heart, "Read it again, child, and then read on."

I started the passage again: "Since, then, you have been raised with Christ, set your hearts on things above, where Christ is seated at the right hand of God. Set your minds on things above, not on earthly things" (3:1-2). I thought, "Both the *mind* and the *heart* are involved. My mental process and thoughts, as well as my emotions and desires. That covers it, doesn't it?"

"For you died, and your life is now hidden with Christ in God" (3:3).

I had to stop there. A prerequisite for focusing on Christ is being dead? When did I die? What does this mean?

I had to look back in chapter two to find out. "When you were dead in your sins and in the uncircumcision of your sinful nature, God made you alive with Christ. He forgave us all our sins, having canceled the written code, with its regulations, that was against us and that stood opposed to us; he took it away, nailing it to the cross" (2:13-14).

A picture flashed across my mind. I stood on a dusty road with a filthy sack on my back, several others in my arms. One sack contained all the regulations of the law that I had failed to uphold. In another sack were the laws I had broken. My old nature with its bad habits, desires, and lusts filled another sack to the top. In the one on my back, the heaviest of all, were the sins I had committed from the day I was born. I staggered beneath my load with no hope, no strength. I was dead inside and almost dead outside.

Then a gentle hand reached for my burden. Carefully He gathered my filthy sacks in His arms. I stood with head bowed in wonder and awe. When I looked up, He was there . . . hanging on a cross. Silhouetted against a forbidding sky, He hung nailed to that cross—and *every one* of my sins was visibly nailed there with Him!

He looked at me and said, "Beloved child, I have paid your penalty. If you receive My gift of dying for you, God will remember your sins no more. They are removed as far as the east from the west, buried in the depths of the deepest sea. You are cleansed. You are alive for eternity."

"For you died . . . ." I died with Christ on that cross as He took all my sins and fastened them there. "And having disarmed the powers and authorities, he made a public spectacle of them, triumphing over them by the cross" (2:15).

When I was about twelve, I knelt with my mother and accepted God's gift of forgiveness. I asked Christ to come into my life and be my Savior. I was already dead spiritually; my sins died with Him so that I might become alive.

Colossians 3:3-4 continues, ". . . and your *life* is now hidden with Christ in God. When Christ, who is your life, appears, then you also will appear with him in glory." Isn't it great that He says we died, but that our *life* is now hidden? We are no longer dead. We are alive! And our life is hidden with Jesus Christ, who is in God. We are doubly protected. Wrapped in His arms. Hidden.

So first of all, we have to *belong* to Christ or else we can never hope to have the ability to focus on Him, nor would we want to. But for us as Christ-ones, all of life, hope, and joy is bound up in setting our minds and hearts on things above—on Him.

Paul gives us further instructions on what to do after we become followers of Christ:

> Put to death, therefore, whatever belongs to your earthly nature: sexual immorality, impurity, lust, evil desires and greed, which is idolatry. Because of these, the wrath of God is coming. You used to walk in these ways, in the life you once lived. But now you must rid yourselves of all such things as these: anger, rage, malice, slander, and filthy language from your lips. Do not lie to each other, since you have taken off your old self with its practices and have put on the new self, which is being renewed in knowledge in the image of its Creator. Here there is no Greek or Jew, circumcised or uncircumcised, barbarian, Scythian, slave or free, but Christ is all, and is in all. (3:5-11).

The Scripture says we are to "put to death" and to "rid" ourselves of all these ugly things in our lives. Even though we have become alive spiritually for all eternity, the old nature of sin needs to be put to death continually in our lives. I couldn't get over the fact that I am to rid *myself* of these things. Oh yes, Christ will constantly help me. God will give me the power. But I am to do it *myself*. My will is involved.

A woman came to a godly friend of mine to ask his advice. She said, "I argue with my mother all the time. We just can't get along. We fight every day. What should I do?"

My friend looked her straight in the eye and said, "Stop it."

Simply stop it! We *choose* to get angry, to have a DRA (in our family that stands for "dirty rotten attitude"). So often we say, "I can't," when really it would be more correct for us to say, "I won't."

A friend of mine said jokingly, "I've saved up all my stress points, so now I *deserve* to have a nervous breakdown!" Well, it is indeed her choice, just as it was Charlie Brown's choice when he said, "I have decided to dread one day at a time."

We have to *will*, to choose, to decide to begin working on putting to death the uglies of our lives. It is our responsibility to make godly decisions.

But God doesn't stop there.

Next we are told to take on godly attitudes:

> Therefore, as God's chosen people, holy and dearly loved, clothe yourselves with compassion, kindness, humility, gentleness and patience. Bear with each other and forgive whatever grievances you may have against one another. Forgive as the Lord forgave you. And over all these virtues put on love, which binds them all together in perfect unity.
>
> Let the peace of Christ rule in your hearts, since as members of one body you were called to peace. And be thankful. (3:12-15)

Aren't you encouraged when you read that your "new self . . . is being renewed in knowledge in the image of its Creator"? This is a maturing process, and a long-term one at that. We have a brand new slate when we receive Christ, but on that slate is constantly being written all our old habits, backgrounds, hang-ups, and the "daily dirt" of ordinary life. So even though we have "put on the new self," we need constant renewal, being cleansed and changed to a true knowledge according to the image of the One who created us.

Joyce Landorf recounts an interesting story of renewal in her book *Changepoints*:

My granddaughter, April Joy, broke a rule at her house the other day. My daughter-in-love, Teresa, caught April in this fractured rule. Then, because Teresa had given birth to Richard Andrew just two months before and the fatigue factor was high, she just let loose with a barrage of shouting and scolding at four-year-old April. Finally, after Teresa had calmed down, after discipline had been administered, and after April's tears had been dried, Teresa had her usual make-up talk and time of setting things aright again. The conversation went something like this:

"April, do you know why Mommie had to punish you?"

"No."

"Well, you broke the rule. That's why."

Sensing that April was still angry about the situation, Teresa asked, "Are you mad at me?"

"Yes," April said soberly.

"But how could you be mad at me? I didn't break the rule—you did!"

Then April said evenly, "I'm mad because you yelled at me, and I'm going to ask God to take the yell out of your face."

Teresa said the soft voice of the Holy Spirit hit her with an incredible blow of conviction. The child was not angry over being punished—it was deserved—but she was hurt and angry about the personal injury of being yelled at.

Here Teresa had been trying to train her child in obedience, and was correct in disciplining her for breaking a rule, but she had lost her self-control (one of the fruits of the Spirit that identifies us as believers), and had carried out the action of discipline with a great deal of unnecessary shouting.

Instantly Teresa said, "Okay, April. You're right about my yelling. Let's pray."

April responded simply, with no malice, forethought, or anger, "Dear Jesus, please take the yell out of Mommie's face, and bless my kitty, Honey. Amen."[1]

As I read this story, I thought, "What a beautiful example of choosing to put on the new self, of being *renewed* in the knowledge of the image of the Creator."

To be renewed—to put on compassion—this too is our choice. Our will is involved in "clothing ourselves," in forgiving, loving, and having the peace of Christ rule in our hearts. We have to put ourselves under that rule.

Compassion is demonstrated in small ways. I love the story of the little boy who had scratched his finger and was trying to show it to his father. Several times the boy attempted to thrust his scratched finger in front of the newspaper his father was reading, and several times he was rebuffed. Finally the father exploded, "Well, I can't do anything about it, can I?" to which the boy replied, "Yes. You could have said, 'Oh!'"

Demonstrating love and compassion is a growing, ongoing process that is learned with time and patience. We will be able to develop these qualities only as we keep our focus on the Lord.

The picture was becoming clearer. I said to the Lord, "All right, Father. I am first of all to be Your child. Next, I am to put off the old things and then put on the new. That sounds great, but I am still wondering *how* I can do all of this."

He said once again, "Read on."

The answer was right before my eyes! A verse I had

memorized way back when, but one I hadn't learned the true significance of: "Let the word of Christ dwell in you richly as you teach and admonish one another with all wisdom, and as you sing psalms, hymns and spiritual songs with gratitude in your hearts to God" (3:16).

Let the word of Christ dwell in you richly. . . . Of course! The way I am going to be able to put off the uglies and put on the beautiful is all wrapped up in letting the word of God dwell deep in my life . . . *richly*. When I hear God's word preached, am I letting it dwell in me at *all*, let alone richly? Do I take notes, go home and think about it, or ask others how they are applying it?

When I am reading the Bible, do I really meditate on it, letting it soak into my soul? Do I underline, write notes about it, keep a daily journal?

When I am studying, am I content with surface answers? Do I just "get by" with my assignment?

When I memorize, do I ask God to penetrate my heart with those truths all day, every day?

And what do I think about during the course of my days? My problems? Imaginations? Or do I meditate and dwell *richly*?

Do I really love God's word? Do I allow it to come to life?

The *key*, the exciting wonderful key to keeping my mind on Christ and on things above, is to let the word dwell in me *richly*, vividly, deeply.

The word of God should flow out from Christ-ones no matter which button is pushed. Our teaching should be seasoned with Scripture, our conversations saturated, our songs vitalized, and every part of our lives infused with praise. But this is possible only when we let the word of God dwell richly within us.

Then as we dwell in God's word, we will be filled to

overflowing with God Himself! That is the immeasurable promise we are given in Scripture:

> When I think of the wisdom and scope of his plan I fall down on my knees and pray . . . that out of his glorious, unlimited resources he will give you the mighty inner strengthening of his Holy Spirit. And I pray that Christ will be more and more at home in your hearts, living within you as you trust in him. May your roots go down deep into the soil of God's marvelous love; and may you be able to feel and understand, as all God's children should, how long, how wide, how deep, and how high his love really is; and to experience this love for yourselves, though it is so great that you will never see the end of it or fully know or understand it. And so at last you will be filled up with God himself. (Ephesians 3:14-19, *The Living Bible*)

What is this swelling crescendo of the Christian life telling us? It tells us that if we are wide open to the Holy Spirit and if we know the love of Christ, which is possible through God's word, we will be *filled* with all the fullness of God.

The secret of victory in the Christian life, the bottom line to glorifying God and enjoying Him forever, is this bounty of grace: knowing the love of Christ until "at last you are filled full with God Himself."

NOTES: 1. Joyce Landorf, *Changepoints*, (Minneapolis: Grason, 1981), pages 35-36.

APPLICATION BIBLE STUDY

1. In what areas do you feel needy right now?

2. (a) Take five minutes to pray for a sensitivity to God's voice speaking to you.

   (b) Read slowly, aloud Colossians 3:1-17.

(c) Reread this passage, stopping at the word or verse that seems to specifically speak to you.

(d) Write out your thoughts about that particular word or verse. What is God saying to you from it? How are you failing to live it? What do you feel God would have you do about it? Be specific.

(e) Memorize Colossians 3:16-17.

3. Another passage to memorize is Ephesians 3:14-20 in *The Living Bible.* This is the key to life—being filled with God!

3
The Measure of Joy

IT WAS AN EPHESIANS 3:20 WEEKEND—all that I could ever have imagined or asked for. God had blessed the conference with a warm, compassionate, exciting group of women, and so I almost floated into the California apartment of my in-laws where I anticipated a boisterous welcome from my loved ones. But as I entered, the empty house wrapped its lonely arms around me. No one was home.

Disappointed, I kicked off my shoes and slung my suitcase on the den hide-a-bed, the balloon of my enthusiasm already pricked.

I contented myself with the Sunday paper, and a few minutes later the family breezed in, tired from a weekend of visiting friends in the desert. I got a casual kiss and a "Hi, how'd it go" before one disappeared into the kitchen, another into the bedroom, and the third—my husband— headed for the phone. A giant hole ruptured, and my balloon went flat. Shreds of self-pity collected at my feet.

Sharing exciting happenings is a natural part of warm relationships. So as soon as Jack was off the phone, he sat down beside me and began to tell me about *his* exciting weekend! I listened, feeling grumpy inside. God had indeed given him some wonderful opportunities to share Christ, some precious new friends, some great highlights from a great weekend. I tried to get excited about his excitement. But I still felt grumpy.

Then he was off again to make another phone call. "Okay," I thought, "if you don't want to hear about what's happened to me, I'll just hibernate." I went into the den, shut the door, and started to read a book.

My thoughts accused me: "Carole, *how could you?* God has just blessed both you *and* Jack in an amazing way, and yet you are now having a dirty rotten attitude. Don't you think you had better practice what you preach?"

I answered myself, "I just don't feel like it! I'm having a private pity-party, and I'd just as soon not break it up, thank you."

A voice sounded somewhere within me: "Carole, this weekend you talked about the fact that joy in one's life is a *choice*, right? That 'you don't feel your way into acting, but you act your way into feeling.' Isn't that true?"

"Don't remind me," I countered. "If I choose to act joyful, then no one will know how terrible I'm really feeling."

"True," came the voice. "But is that more important than obeying Me?"

Just then my silent conversation was interrupted by

Jack coming into the den, asking me if there was something wrong. Bless him. He is so sensitive.

And then we *did* talk. He listened and rejoiced with me. My excitement inflated again from his careful attention.

So I never did find out who was going to win: my unreasonable attitude or the still, insistent voice of God. Once again God had provided a "way of escape" for me. But even as He was providing that escape, He was bringing to mind a curious scene. . . .

***

I was in the car driving toward the Celestial City. Two roads headed that way, with frequent cross-overs. But Highway One, the road I had chosen, was a lulu! I sighed as the heavily loaded tractor trailers in front of me caused traffic to go so slowly. The long tunnels were pitch black and scary. Construction was frequent and detours abounded. The intense noise level gave me an Excedrin headache.

I hunched up my aching back as I thought, "This is the pits! I'd sure like to leave this ugly road!" Although there were many trucks and cars, I knew I couldn't count on the occupants to stop if I had a flat or got stuck in the mud. Each person was concentrating solely on the arduous task of driving. I thought, "What a bunch of negative people," and then I remembered what E. Stanley Jones said:

> The mood of the present day is cynicism. Many people are soured on life. They are cynical and negative. This age has three sneers for everything and three cheers for nothing. . . . They are trying to live by a No. And it is turning out badly and sadly, for you can't live by a No. You have to live by a Yes.

Bertrand Russell said that life is a bottle of very nasty wine that leaves a bad taste in your mouth. A great actor was dying and said, "Let down the curtain, the farce is over. There is no reality in life; it is a farce." Sartre, the French existentialist, said, "Hell is other people." How can you have a society if you believe other people are hell?[1]

As a truck stopped suddenly in front of me, I slammed on my brakes. To my astonishment, the truck backed up a few feet (my hand was pressed desperately on the horn, but it didn't even phase him), tilted and opened the bed, and proceeded to dump his load of dirt all over my car. Then he drove away without looking back. I spent the next few hours digging out.

It was then that I decided I'd had enough of Highway One, so I edged over to the nearest crossover. This other road looked less traveled and without so many potholes. As I exited, suddenly I found myself in the passenger's seat. Someone else was driving, someone I recognized!

He smiled and said, "You don't mind if I drive, do you? I'm a little tired of sitting in the back seat."

I stammered in confusion, "I . . . I need all the help I can get!" And inwardly I thought, "I didn't even realize You were riding with me."

"You've had a hard time on the other highway," He continued. (As if I didn't know!) "I don't understand why you wanted to keep driving, why you didn't ask for My help."

He paused, but I decided that whatever I said would be wrong, so I kept silent.

"Each person has a choice of roads to travel. No matter which road you take to the City, it will have some difficult spots. Highway One is exhausting when you try to drive it by yourself. And most people act like I'm not even there." (Whoops—He knew!) "I watched that truck dump its load on you—that was a heavy one, wasn't it?" He continued in a companionable way. "Truthfully, I was surprised that you didn't ask Me to help you dig out from under. But then, a lot of people don't. If they did, I could clear that rubbish up in a minute." I thought, "A *minute*? I spent hours, and still the car isn't clean."

"I was also amazed that you didn't ask Me about the construction and detours. If you had, I'd have advised you to change roads long ago. But you, like a lot of My friends, seem to prefer to grumble and complain about the condition of the road, about your loneliness in driving, rather than asking Me for help."

His voice trailed off sadly. But then He smiled as He said, "I'm glad you decided to change roads. You are now on Route Seven; this highway's name is Joy. I'll gladly be your Driver and teach you some wonderful things along the way. We will also see some spectacular scenery together." I liked that word "together."

"After what I've been through, I'd really appreciate that," I said hesitatingly. "But shouldn't I drive?"

"Against the rules," He said. "I'm the only Driver allowed on this highway. I know every curve, every tunnel, every dangerous spot. But if you want to, you can change over to the other route at any time and drive."

"Thank you, but I think I'd like to stay on this one, Lord."

"Good," He approved. Then abruptly He asked, "Are you hungry? There's some food in the back seat."

Hungry was an understatement. I was starved! So I reached for this huge basket, and under the cloth I discovered the most savory morsels I'd ever seen.

"What a feast!" I exclaimed. And into my heart came the verse, "[We] feast on the abundance of your house [and] drink from your river of delights" (Psalm 36:8).

It was while I was eating that I became aware of a Song. The music made me smile, even as we came to a forbidding tunnel. It looked just as dark and menacing as the ones I'd gone through on the other road.

My Driver knew what I was thinking. "Don't worry," He said. "This is a rather long tunnel we are coming to. It's name is Illness. But go through the tunnel and see what happens."

We entered the sinister opening. But as soon as we were in it, the tunnel was illuminated. And then I realized that the light was coming from my Driver! The tunnel—though I still preferred the sunshine—was a new opportunity to see His skill. So certain. So expert. And all the while, He was teaching me astonishing things about the very tunnel we were going through.

"Remember the verse that says, 'Consider it pure joy when all kinds of trials and temptations come into your life'? Let Me explain what that really means. We are going to be passing through several tunnels on our way to the City. Some are designed just for your personal journey, but most of them are tunnels that everyone has to go through. We are also going to travel valleys of death, cross bridges of broken relationships, and wind our way through forests of pain.

"The road you just left, Highway One, is really not much different from this one as far as the territory to be covered. Of course, you can get yourself into a lot of trouble over there running into ditches, detours, and accidents. But those are selfmade difficulties, not a part of the road itself. As I said, the territory to be covered is much the same, but the similarity ends right there. On this road I do the driving, so you can just sit back and relax. I will fill the valleys with sunshine, the forests with fruit, the highway and dark tunnels with light. As I show you My treasures, that Song you have been hearing very faintly in the background will grow continually stronger.

"But the verse that begins, 'Consider it pure joy,' means that you have the choice. At any moment you can choose to go back to the other road. There you will drive and the tunnels will be dark. The Song will be silenced.

"The personal results of choosing Highway Joy will be maturity and completeness."

He paused, and then He said softly, "I wonder why so many people choose that other highway."

When we finally made it through the tunnel, we stopped briefly to pick up some friends. They were filled with stories of how God had been working in their lives. As they talked, the Song became more audible and distinct.

When at last they got out of the car to resume their journey, my Driver said, "Joy can always be found as God works in the lives of His people." Just then I remembered the thankfulness of David as he wrote, "The Lord has done great things for us, and we are filled with joy" (Psalm 126:3).

My Driver was silent for some time, so I watched the scenery for a while. Then, just as I was getting tired, we pulled alongside a stream where some people were having a picnic. They shared all they had with me, and when it was time to go, they gave me a hug of encouragement. As I climbed back into the car, I glanced back to see a banner hanging over the picnic grounds, which read, "A man finds joy in giving an apt reply—and how good is a timely word!" (Proverbs 15:23). The Song swelled in my ears.

I determined at that moment never to travel that other road.

And yet a few days later that was exactly where I was. Driving myself. Back behind a load of problems, off into a rut of fear, detoured by worry. My Song gone.

"Help!" I cried. "I can't seem to find the way back

to Highway Joy. I'm desperate. I don't like this *one bit!"*

And suddenly, without even consciously finding a crossover, I was on that golden road, a passenger once again, with my Driver in control.

"What happened? What went wrong?" I asked Him. "I really didn't mean to get back on Highway One. Why did I?"

"My friend, your problem is that you look around you too much—and at all the wrong things! Instead of keeping your eyes on the City and on the treasures I have been pointing out to you, you got distracted and veered off to the other road."

"What can I do to prevent that?" I asked.

"I've already given you a Helper," my Driver said. "But so far you haven't seemed to notice Him."

It was then that I became conscious of a wonderful Being riding with us—strong, full of power.

"Years ago when I lived on the earth," my Driver said, "I told My disciples, 'You will weep and mourn while the world rejoices. You will grieve, but your grief will turn to joy . . . when the Holy Spirit comes.' (John 16:20). My Spirit will always be with you, ready to respond to your cry at any moment. He is the One who transferred you to this road when you cried for help. Count on Him!"

And so my Song grew and was magnified so much that its consuming wonder filled my heart and my life. With my eyes straight ahead toward the "things above," with the power and help of the Holy Spirit, with my confidence in the Driver of my life, I could stay on Highway Joy. And the words rang in my ears: "This is the victory that has overcome the world, even our faith. Who is it that overcomes the world? Only he who believes that Jesus is the Son of God" (1 John 5:4-5).

***

The picture faded, but the truth remained sharply in focus. I can dwell crushed under the mountain of my problems and my circumstances, or I can *choose* to consider them joy, and then be freed to soar above those very difficulties. Always I am held safely in the refuge of His wings.

NOTES: 1. E. Stanley Jones, *The Divine Yes* (New York: Pillar Books, 1975), pages 14-15.

APPLICATION BIBLE STUDY

1. What to you is the difference between happiness and joy?

2. Think back over this week and list times you were *happy*. What contributed to your happiness? List people or events that have given you joy this week. If your list is short, can you explain what is lacking in you? Where can you seek help?

3. Read Galatians 5:22-23. What do you think it means when the Scripture says that joy is a fruit of the Spirit?

4. According to the Bible, what are some things that give us joy? Psalm 16:8-9; Proverbs 12:25; Proverbs 23:24; Acts 16:34; Romans 14:17-18; 2 John 12.

Seeing God work in the lives of ones we love adds to our joy. Indeed, just *seeing* those people brings joy. As a grandmother who only gets to see her grandchildren and children once or twice a year (they live in Mexico as missionaries), I can attest to this fact fervently! Paul said of Timothy, "Recalling your tears, I long to see you, so that I may be filled with joy" (2 Timothy 1:4). Seeing my Timothy (isn't it special that God gave us a son-in-law with that name?), my Lynn, Eric (age 5½), and Sunny (age 2½) fills *me* with joy, too.

Have you ever prayed to be able to see friends and loved ones? You shouldn't eat your heart out when you can't, but have you ever asked God for the *joy* of visits with special ones and let Him open up the time in

His own miraculous way? Sometimes we don't have because we don't *ask*. Paul continually prayed to see ones he cared for.

5. Memorize Psalm 126:3 or one of the other verses from this chapter that has been significant to you.

4
Growing in Joy

M Y MOTHER LOOKED AT the doctor in desperation. "What can I do?" she asked. "When my baby gets angry, she holds her breath until she turns blue. I'm afraid she'll hurt herself."

The doctor shook his head and smiled. "Don't worry about it. If she holds her breath until she loses consciousness, she'll automatically begin to breathe again. She can't kill herself that way."

That doctor was one wise man. Nevertheless, when I would lose control of my temper as a child and bang my head against a wall, Mother was concerned. As I grew older, my parents put parameters on how I could express my anger. I could not strike anyone, scream, swear, or throw things. So my fury was vented by stomping up the stairs, slamming the door at the top as hard as I could, banging the bedroom door even harder, and then sobbing hysterically until I was exhausted.

When Jack and I got married and moved into a twenty-eight-foot trailer that had a sliding door into the tiny bedroom, Mom often commented on how difficult it would be without a door for me to slam. But by then God had done some work in my life.

Scripture tells us, "Everyone should be quick to listen, slow to speak and slow to become angry, for man's anger does not bring about the righteous life that God desires" (James 1:19-20). For many years that was *not* a picture of my life. And there are still times when a snapshot of my life would not measure up. But God and I are working on it.

However, before I was ready to deal with specific commands on anger, God had to bring me back to the book of James. When you think of the first chapter of James, what do *you* think of? Suffering, right? Or do you think of the double-minded man? Well, let me contribute another thought.

It's about *joy*. Yes, it really is.

I'm sure that the picture-allegory in the previous chapter popped into my head because I had been studying James at the time. The initial lesson that James gives us is that we *choose* whether or not we will live under our problems or above them. We are responsible for our actions. "When all kinds of trials and temptations crowd into your lives, my brothers, don't resent them as intruders, but welcome them as friends! Realise that they come to test your faith and to produce in you the quality of endurance. But let the process go on until that endurance is fully developed, and you will find you have become men of mature character, men of integrity with no weak spots" (James 1:2-4, *Phillips*).

That's what I need: the quality of endurance, fully developed, which leads to a mature character. And how is this accomplished? Through trials and temptations. (I don't *like* it, but that's what it says.) Trials are friends in disguise.

Have you been welcoming any trials lately? I have to admit, that's hard for me to do. My "resentment" level gets pretty high sometimes.

Now how can I actually consider it joy when difficulties invade my life? What can I do to ensure that my life will be full of joy? God gives several "how-to's" that, if practiced, will fill us with His music to the limit of our capacity. We may hear the strain of the Song faintly or perhaps with great reverberation in our ears: it all depends on the amount and depth of our receiving.

God tells us to "consider it joy" when we are faced with difficulties. He *commands* it. And if He commands it, He Himself by the power of His Holy Spirit will give us the ability to do it. But *how*?

The word

God's word will fill us with joy. Jesus said to His disciples, "I have told you this so that my joy may be in you and that your joy may be complete" (or full) (John 15:11). Behind that statement are all the precious things He has told us about heaven, abiding in Him, and spiritual fruit. All the wonderful truths He has shared—His very own word—are bound to fill us with joy.

And it is true. The difference between having a little joy or being filled up with joy lies in how much or how little we are willing to settle for. If we sip shallowly, we will have shallow joy. If we drink deeply, letting His word quench our spiritual thirst with refreshing water, then we will be filled with joy.

When was the last time you were so filled with joy from reading the promises of God that inside you were jumping up and down and clapping your emotional hands? God wants to flood our hearts with overwhelming joy from His word. *But* we first have to ask Him for that joy, beginning with expectancy and then digging for the treasures. We have to be willing to spend the time and energy to dwell richly in His presence.

The story is told of a gifted concert violinist who was complimented after the conclusion of a particularly moving performance.

"That was absolutely wonderful," said the admirer. "I'd give my life to be able to play like that."

"I did," replied the artist.[1]

It takes commitment to be filled with joy. It takes the dedication of your whole life.

A focus on results

If we want to consider our trials with a joyful attitude, we must keep our eyes on the end results. There *is* a purpose for all the trials that God allows to crowd into my life. The purpose has to do with a quality of life—a honing of my character, a perfecting of the inner *me*, who needs much improvement. If I can see beyond the circumstances to the end results, then joy will ensue. And what results there are! Only one is described in James, but what a fantastic one it is. The testing of our faith develops perseverance, and perseverance, when it has chipped away at us long enough, is going to make us mature—complete. Through this growing process, we will become men and women of mature character.

In *Discovering God's Will*, a study book by Warren

and Ruth Myers, this truth is aptly stated: "Often we feel we know better than God what is good for us. To some of us, . . . it means getting what we think we want, when we want it. We want what brings a present sense of pleasure, relief or achievement. God also cares about our present joy, but even more he wants to ripen our capacity for enjoyment in every aspect of our person. He wants us to learn happiness not governed by what happens in our lives, a stable happiness that is not always threatened. He wants us to go beyond the dribbles of satisfaction we can force out of life."[2]

This happiness is not "governed by what happens in our lives"; it will never occur apart from difficult lessons in God's school.

If we keep our eyes on the end results of all the lessons, we can take the tests with joy, work on the exams with patience, labor over our term papers with perseverance and gladness. Amy Carmichael writes about such a positive attitude:

> The son prayed, Be not far from me, for trouble is near, and his thoughts said, How can one be glad or even peaceful when trouble is near?
>
> His Father said, Before thy Saviour went to Bethany, when trouble was near, He was peaceful; and He said to His disciples, I am glad. For He looked not at the things that are seen, but at the things which are not seen. Canst thou not do likewise?
>
> Look through the approaching trouble, whatever it be, to that which is beyond it. Then thou wilt find that thou canst be peaceful, and even be able to say, "I am glad." For the Lord sitteth above the water-flood and the Lord remaineth a King forever. The Lord shall give strength unto His people: the Lord shall give His people the blessing of peace.[3]

Obedience

If we do what God says, we will have joy. "Blessed [happy] is the man who perseveres under trial, because when he has stood the test, he will receive the crown of life that God has promised to those who love him" (James 1:12).

Maturing through the trial of my temper—persevering by biting my tongue when I feel like unleashing it, counting to ten when I want to explode, disciplining myself by sticking to the conflict instead of digging up the past (whenever I do these things)—has not only helped in my "growing up," but it has given me true *joy*.

***

As you consider the importance of being filled with joy, remember that joy is not a feeling, (although when you practice choosing joy, a feeling of joy will eventually come). Remember the statement, "You don't feel your way into acting; you act your way into feeling." Exactly. It is true with love in a marriage; it is true with cheerfulness in the home; it is true with joy in our lives. When we obey *anyhow*, the feeling of joy will follow.

But obedience must stand all by itself with or without feeling. Betty Elliot says, "God allows the absence of feeling or, more often, the presence of strong negative feeling that we may simply follow, simply obey, simply trust."[4]

With this in mind we have to commit ourselves to *choose joy without feeling it.* Then we must trust God to control the heart's responses in His time.

I love this thought given by God to Amy Carmichael:

> His thoughts said, I do not understand how such gladness as this that is given can be when nothing that I expected is happening, and much that I hoped would never happen has been allowed to come.

For a while his Father was silent in His love, and the son was silent too. At last he thought he heard these words: It is written of thy dear Lord, "Thy God hath anointed Thee with the Oil of Gladness." With a little of that blessed Oil He hath anointed even thee. And then—and this was a word of wonder to the son—his Father said clearly, *I thank thee for thy joy.*[5]

Amazing thought. Our joy brings joy to the Father.

These are relative measures of joy. But God wants to give us even more than a measure. He wants us to be *filled to overflowing*, and so again I pray, "Lord, keep showing me *how.*"

NOTES: 1. *Reader's Digest*, December 1981.
         2. Warren and Ruth Myers, *Discovering God's Will* (Colorado Springs: NavPress, 1980), page 5.
         3. Amy Carmichael, *His Thoughts Said, His Father Said* (Fort Washington, PA: Christian Literature Crusade), pages 81-82).
         4. Elisabeth Elliot, *Love Has a Price Tag* (Chappaqua, NY: Christian Herald Books, 1979), page 140.
         5. Carmichael, *His Thoughts*, page 99.

APPLICATION BIBLE STUDY

1. Many things will and can bring us joy, but what is *the* essential factor for having joy according to Psalm 16:11, John 3:29-30, and Acts 13:52?

2. Write out John 15:11 in your own words. What is Christ referring to as "this"? How, practically, can this give us joy? Give an example from your own life of how the words of Christ have given you real joy.

3. Read John 16:24. When was the last time an answer to prayer brought you fullness of joy? Are you satisfied with the joy that comes from your prayer life? What do you think God wants you to do to improve your communication with Him?

One of the many reasons why we fail to get excited about prayer is that we've lost one of the foundations of joy. When was the last time you were excited about the fact of your salvation? A year or so ago, Psalm 51:12 jumped out of the page at me as I was praying about joy. "Restore to me the joy of your salvation and grant me a willing spirit, to sustain me." How basic!

In the same week I read Luke 10:18-22, which tells how excited Christ's disciples were when demons submitted to them in Christ's name. Christ was glad, too, but said, "However, do not rejoice that the spirits submit to you, but rejoice that your names are written in heaven." I don't think Christ was telling the disciples not to be happy about how they were being used to promote His kingdom. But He was saying, "Let's get down to fundamentals. The foremost reason to rejoice is that you are one of Mine. Rejoice in your salvation." If we are doing this, then our joy will remain when the circumstances of life are grim as well as when they are grand.

4. Both Scripture and answered prayer bring joy, according to John 15:11 and 16:24. Write out a statement of how these two gifts help us to be "filled with God Himself"—the source of the fullness of joy.

5. Memorize Psalm 16:11 and think about it this week.

5
Filled with Joy

A SMALL CARD tacked to my cork pen-holder reads:

> JOY
> is the flag flown
> from the castle
> when the King is in residence!

". . . when the King is in *residence!*" Not a guest in the residence, but *fully occupied* by Him. When our lives are saturated with the Triune God, our joy will be full.[1] I need this reminder often: joy comes from, resides in, and is all wrapped up in God alone.

I almost came up out of my chair one day when I was

reading Proverbs. It had been a rather ordinary day in an ordinary week in an ordinary month. But Proverbs 8:30-31 showed me how an ordinary day can become extraordinary: "I was filled with delight day after day, rejoicing always in his presence, rejoicing in his whole world and delighting in mankind."

In the context, the "I" is Wisdom, which is a picture of Christ. Because Christ lives in me (Galatians 2:20), this passage in Proverbs should be a description of me. We are told of three things that will fill us with delight.

The first focus of our rejoicing is *being in His presence,* We are told to delight in God Himself. If we don't delight in Him, we will be unable to delight in the other two areas.

In the midst of Job's despair, he glanced back over his shoulder to picture for us the love and blessing of God on his life. What a scene—basking in the warmth of God's intimate love. Job said, "God watched over me, . . . his lamp shone upon my head and by his light I walked through darkness! . . . God's intimate friendship blessed my house, . . . my path was drenched with cream" (Job 29:2-6).

Don't you love that? "His path was drenched with cream"! How often do you and I feel this way? If not, could it be that we are not sensitive to God's blessings—not looking for them, praying for them? I'm not talking about material blessings, but the riches of His grace.

Our second focus is *rejoicing in His whole world.* I must admit that this isn't hard to do in Colorado Springs. Today is a day I wish I could capture on paper, xeroxing about 362 days a year just like it (365 might get a bit monotonous). Deep blue sky, snow-capped Pikes Peak, seventy degrees, crystal clear air. In my walk this morning, I had to spend most of my time just praising God for His world. But even in Colorado—and in spite of God answering my prayer of ten years ago, which was, "Lord, help me never to take this beauty for granted"—I often fail to delight in His world. I don't take the time to examine the beauty of the flowers, to observe the sunsets, to wriggle my toes in the grass, to heed the soft music of rain on the leaves, or to appreciate God's deep bass organ of thunder.

God Himself expressed delight in His world, rejoicing in how "the morning stars sang together" and how He had "given order to the morning [and] shown the dawn its place, that it might take the earth by the edges and shake the wicked out of it" (Job 38:7,12-13).

How long has it been since you delighted in the morning stars while they were singing like a choir? When was the last time you got up expressly to see the dawn being shown its place by God?

I was awed by a letter written from Jesse Brand, a pioneer missionary in India, to his son, Paul. Living in the most primitive conditions, enduring hardships we cannot imagine, separated from his son and daughter, he wrote:

> Yesterday when I was riding over the wind-swept hilltops around Kulivalavu, I could not help thinking of an old hymn that begins, "Heaven above is deeper blue, flowers with purer beauty glow." When I am alone on these long rides, I just love the sweet-smelling world, the dear brown earth, the lichen on the rocks, the heaps of dead brown leaves drifted like snow in the hollows. God means us to delight in his world. Just observe. Remember. Compare. And be always looking to God with thankfulness and worship for having placed you in such a delightful corner of the universe as Planet Earth.[2]

If I stopped regularly to ask God for an attitude of appreciation that is due His world, I would become far more delighted. I need to work on this one.

Our third focus is *delighting in mankind.*

I wonder how many of us divide the people we know into two categories—those we can delight in (grandchildren, for sure!) and those we can't. We usually concentrate our thinking on those we can't.

But more and more I am realizing that God wants me to rejoice in all (well, most, anyway) of mankind—certainly in those He has called to be His children. In order to do this, I must practice Philippians 4:8: "Fix your thoughts on what is true and good and right. Think about things that are pure and lovely, and dwell on the fine, good things in others. Think about all you can praise God for and be glad about" (*The Living Bible*).

the glad game

It is easy to be negative. In one family survey parents were asked to record how many negative—as opposed to positive—comments they made to their children. Results: they criticized ten times for every favorable comment. In a survey in Orlando, Florida, teachers were found to be seventy-five percent negative. It was learned also that it takes four positive statements from a teacher to offset the effects of one negative statement to a child.[3]

We often think about the negative characteristics in other people or the things they have done to hurt us. In my case especially, the negative things in *me* (and there are many) often oppress me. But I must remember that I, too, am one of God's special creatures. I need to practice Philippians 4:8 in my thoughts about others *and* myself.

Thinking about Proverbs 8:30-31, I asked myself, "How often do I deliberately stop the flow of negative thoughts and determine to think only what is true and right and good?" (Answer: not often enough.) "How often do I 'delight' in mankind?" (Answer: maybe once a month, if I'm lucky.) Yet this is what Wisdom does. This is what Christ does. This is what I, with Christ living in me, should do also—and I can, with His strength and help.

Joy comes from deliberately choosing, as an act of my will, to delight in God, His world, and His people. Joy also comes from seeing God invade His world and His people through His answers to our cries.

I am convinced that much of our lives are dull and boring instead of full and rewarding because we fail to invite God to become a part of the dailies. God tells us to ask Him . . . He all but begs us to ask Him . . . He *commands* us to ask Him. But we don't. Much of our life is lived as though He were not around. Christ promised joy when He said, "Until now you have not asked for anything in my name. Ask and you will receive, and your joy will be complete" (John 16:24).

When I read the bumper sticker—"You are children of God. Please call home"—I grinned and "called home" right on the spot. But friends, I shouldn't need such a reminder to pray *without ceasing*—to be continually asking my Father to be involved in even the smallest details of my life.

Yes, at times it is work to pray. And again, it is a choice. Our *wills* are involved.

J. Sidlow Baxter makes an excellent point when he says, "Most of us need to lift our prayer life from the tyranny of our moods." He then talks about a time when he had allowed prayer to get crowded out of his life. He would repent, try again, fail, confess, and then the whole process would be repeated. One day he had to face up to his own nature. He recounts this inner struggle in a fascinating allegory:

> I'm not the introspective type, but that morning I took a good look into Sidlow Baxter. And I found that there was an area of me that did not want to pray. I had to admit it. It didn't want to pray. But I looked more closely and I found that there was a part of me that did. The part that

didn't was the emotions, and the part that did was the intellect and the will.

Suddenly I found myself asking Sidlow Baxter: "Are you going to let your will be dragged about by your changeful emotions?" And I said to my will: "Will, are you ready for prayer?" And Will said, "Here I am, I'm ready." So I said, "Come on, Will, we will go."

So Will and I set off to pray. But the minute we turned our footsteps to go and pray all my emotions began to talk: "We're not coming, we're not coming, we're not coming." And I said to Will, "Will, can you stick it?" And Will said, "Yes, if you can." So Will and I, we dragged off those wretched emotions and we went to pray, and stayed an hour in prayer.

If you had asked me afterwards, Did you have a good time, do you think I could have said yes? A good time? No, it was a fight all the way.

What I would have done without the companionship of Will, I don't know. In the middle of the most earnest intercessions I suddenly found one of the principal emotions way out on the golf course, playing golf. And I had to run to the golf course and say, "Come back." . . . It was exhausting, but we did it.

The next morning came. I looked at my watch and it was time. I said to Will, "Come on, Will, it's time for prayer." And all the emotions began to pull the other way and I said, "Will, can you stick it?" And Will said, "Yes, in fact I think I'm stronger after the struggle yesterday morning." So Will and I went in again.

The same thing happened. Rebellious, tumultuous, uncooperative emotions. If you had asked me, "Have you had a good time?" I would have had to tell you with tears, "No, the heavens were like brass. It was a job to concentrate. I had an awful time with the emotions."

This went on for about two and a half weeks. But Will and I stuck it out. Then one morning during that third week I looked at my watch and I said, "Will, it's time for prayer. Are you ready?" And Will said, "Yes, I'm ready."

And just as we were going in I heard one of my chief emotions say to the others, "Come on, fellows, there's no use wearing ourselves out: they'll go on whatever we do."

That morning we didn't have any hilarious experience or wonderful visions. . . . But Will and I were able with less distraction to get on with praying. And that went on for another two or three weeks. In fact, Will and I had begun to forget the emotions. . . .

Suddenly one day while Will and I were pressing our case at the throne of the heavenly glory one of the chief emotions shouted "Hallelujah!" and all the other emotions suddenly shouted "Amen!" For the first time the whole territory of James Sidlow Baxter was happily coordinated in the exercise of prayer, and God suddenly became real and heaven was wide open and Christ was there and the Holy Spirit was moving and I knew that all the time God had been listening.[4]

Mr. Baxter's story is mine. Prayer is work. Of course it should be the most joyful, wonderful work that a Christian can be involved in. After all, we are talking to the King of kings and the Lord of lords—personally, on a face-to-face basis, because of our forgiveness by the blood of Jesus Christ.

But our human nature being what it is, the world and its temptations being what they are, the pressures of society, the busy-ness of our days—negative factors such as these rob us quite often of the joy of the act of praying itself. And that is where Will comes in. And Will needs to keep coming in until the joy returns—joy first of all in the actual time we spend praying, and then in God's answers.

To be filled with joy: to see God's miracles in our lives and in the lives of those we love; to know that God is involved in the dailies of our lives; to comprehend that His love, His interest, and His guidance give us joy without measure; to delight in His presence, His world, and His people in our hearts; to be flooded with the truths of His word; to know the end results of the trials of this life, thus making them all worthwhile.

Fullness of joy.

Someone asked a Christian, "If I accept your Jesus Christ, what will happen to me?"

The answer was, "You will stumble upon wonder after wonder, and every wonder will be true!"[5]

His thoughts said, The way is rough.

His Father said, But every step bringeth thee nearer
   to thy Home.

His thoughts said, The fight is fierce.

His Father said, He who is near to his Captain is sure to be a
   target for the archers.

His thoughts said, The night is long.

His Father said, But joy cometh in the morning.

                                        Amy Carmichael

NOTES: 1. Our joy will be full as we rejoice in all three persons of the Godhead:
         The Father: David exulted, "You have made known to me the path of life; you will fill me with joy in your presence, with eternal pleasures at your right hand" (Psalm 16:11).
         The Son: John the Baptist said of Christ, "The friend who attends the bridegroom waits and listens for him, and is full of joy when he hears the bridegroom's voice. That joy is mine, and it is now complete" (John 3:29). Peter testified, "Though you have not seen him, you love him; and even though you do not see him now, you believe in him and are filled with an inexpressible and glorious joy" (1 Peter 1:8). And Christ Himself promised, as He prayed for His disciples and all believers, "I say these things while I am still

in the world, so that they may have the full measure of my joy
within them" (John 17:13).
The Holy Spirit: Joy is coupled throughout the New Testament
with being filled with the Spirit (Acts 13:52, Luke 10:21). Joy
is a fruit of the Holy Spirit (Galatians 5:22).

2. Gladys Hunt, "Evelyn Harris Brand," *Bright Legacy* (Ann Arbor: Servant Books, 1983), page 136.
3. *Christian Digest*, February 1977.
4. J. Sidlow Baxter, "Will and Emotions," *Decision*, July 1972. Reprinted by permission of J. Sidlow Baxter.
5. Anne Ortland, *Acts of Joanna* (Waco: Word Books, 1982), page 63.

APPLICATION BIBLE STUDY

1. Do you think it is possible to be filled with joy all the time? Explain your answer.

2. What do Psalm 36:7-8 and Jude 24-25 say about being filled with joy?

3. According to the following verses, what must we do to have true joy?
   (a) Psalm 27:6 *trust, sacrifice of praise*
   (b) Psalm 43:4-5 *God is the source –*
   (c) Habakkuk 3:17-19
   (d) Hebrews 12:2 *stay hopeful – look beyond circumstances*
   (e) Hebrews 12:15 *forgiveness (stay in fellowship)*
   (f) James 1:2-5

4. What steps do you need to take this week toward joy? Make a list for each day and review it early in the day.

5. Memorize and meditate on one of the above passages that was meaningful to you.

Our will is involved – its a choice to have joy

Keep a praise journal

6
Filled with Praise

*Her thoughts said, You have told me that I should be filled
with praise. My soul is greatly lacking in gladness. Teach
me Thy way.*

*Her Father said, One of the ways the soul is supplied
with delight is by seeing Me work in the events of those
you love. Watch and see.*

THE DAY BEGAN with small stirrings of sound. I heard voices
murmuring, water running, Gonzo (the dog of fifty-
seven varieties) pattering across the tile floor. The small den
hide-a-bed creaked as I stirred. It was 5:30 A.M., and I
opened my eyes reluctantly—then came awake, fully alert.
I poked my head out of the red-curtained doorway and in-
quired, "Is this it?"

Quickly Lynn and her husband Tim replied in unison, "Yes, this is it!"

I had arrived in quaint Guanajuato, Mexico two days before, timing my arrival shortly before Lynn's due date for grandchild number two. Eric, age three, would need watching while Lynn was at the hospital. I'd had thirty-six hours to visit them and to become acquainted with their third-floor apartment before this early hour on May 21.

Shortly after Lynn went into the tiny bathroom, we heard a frantic scream. "Help! The baby's coming! I can't get off the toilet!"

Tim and I rushed in to see Lynn arching her back and hanging on to a towel bar with a desperate grip.

"We can't make it to the doctor's or the hospital!" she wailed.

Tim rushed for the phone. Hastily, he called a friend to go after the doctor. (The doctor didn't have a phone.)

Gone were our original plans to pick up Solita, the "Lamaze coach," to fetch the doctor, and to journey on to the hospital. In fifteen seconds all our best-laid plans were erased.

"Get a sheet!" yelled Tim, so I grabbed one off the hide-a-bed. "We'll try to get her to the den."

But Lynn couldn't move that ten-foot distance! So Tim eased her to the tile floor of the bathroom, deftly sliding the sheet under her and cushioning her head with a couple of pillows. Because her body blocked the door of the tiny bathroom, I couldn't even get in to hold her head.

Tim was trying to do three things at once—call for help via the telephone (I can't speak Spanish), hold Lynn's arms while she was having almost constant contractions, and deliver his own child into the world.

Lynn's cries had awakened Eric, who appeared at his bedroom door wide-eyed and frightened. I tried to keep him in his room, but he'd have none of that. He was crying for his Daddy (who was very busy at the moment). Finally, I got him settled on the hide-a-bed, caring also for bewildered Gonzo.

I felt helpless—not even being able to answer the phone for Tim. When it rang, I answered and yelled frantically, "I don't know! Just HURRY!"

Tim was magnificent . . . and Lynn a brave trooper. At one point I peered in to see a tiny crack of blood and flesh emerging. Tim feared that the cord had wrapped itself around the head, but as he gently pushed with his finger he was greatly relieved to find it hard—like a head, not a cord.

I left to tend Eric, boil water, and keep watch at the window for the appearance of the doctor, praying constantly. A scream from Lynn, a cry from Tim, "*Push*, it's coming!" And then I rushed around the corner to see a bloody head emerging, looking dead and somehow not human. I drew in my breath with concern.

Then a thrilling sound—a tiny cry from the baby even *before* being completely out. The infant was alive!

One final push as Tim turned the shoulders slightly. And then he was shouting and laughing, "It's a girl!" A moment of wild euphoria with Lynn laughing half hysterically but genuinely, "Praise God! It's a girl! It's a girl! Mom, we've got a girl! We've got a baby!"

Tim placed the baby, bloody mucous and all, on Lynn's stomach. Just then I looked out the window to see a woman arriving in a car. "Up here!" I shouted. It was a friend, Eva, who was a nurse. She calmly took over and tied the cord with Tim's new shoe laces, cut it with sterilized kitchen shears, delivered the placenta (keeping it for examination), and washed the baby with the water I'd boiled (my minor contribution).

Immediately—or so it seemed—the apartment was filled

with ten people, including two doctors, one a close friend. In the confusion, Lynn was left alone until she hollered, "Hey, I'm over here!"

Lynn wanted her father to know immediately, so I called Jack at about 7:00 A.M. He said to me later, "I have never heard you sound so *shook*."

Then we managed to get Lynn down two flights of stairs and into the VW van. A friend took Eric for the day. I held the baby as we followed the doctor into downtown Guanajuato.

I was beginning to "come to"—to be less in a state of shock—as we stopped at a hospital you just wouldn't believe: yellow stucco, peeling paint, flush to the sidewalk; no wheelchairs, emergency room, or nurses to help. Lynn walked in and we, stumbling under a load of suitcase, shoulder bag, and baby, tried to help her.

Lynn was helped on to a table in the surgery department. She needed a general anesthetic, because she had to be sewn up from tears both inside and out.

So Tim and I went into the hallway to wait, as a man disinfected the floor in continuous slow motion.

This hospital was the closest one to their apartment—a socialized-medicine government hospital like nothing I'd ever seen before. Green tile walls, green and white linoleum worn to the bare cement in spots, dark narrow hallways. Tim checked out the toilets and said tersely, "Don't go."

No food or beverages were available at the hospital, and there was no place close by to get any. Rusted cabinets containing absolutely nothing stood by each of the six beds in the dormitory-style recovery room—a stark, dark room with one window at the far end. Blood-stained sheets were still on the bed next to Lynn's. There were no pans for the patients. Post-operative patients were wheeled in—relatives trailing behind to look out for them. A tiny Indian lady, a long black braid down her back, stood by her unconscious daughter who had been injured in a fall. The mother was dressed in an inside-out red sweater over a flowered dress with a bright pink apron. She bent over Lynn's bed for a time, then sat on the floor by her daughter.

A woman squatted on the hall floor, separating tortillas to sell to the nurses.

And the cleaning man kept mopping the hall with the strong disinfectant.

Five uncomfortable straight-back chairs lined the hallway where we waited. For six eternal hours I continued to hug the baby close in my arms, except for a brief time when she was taken to be weighed and footprinted. Tim signed the birth certificate, officially naming her Sonya Marie Westberg.

Finally the doctor came back to release Lynn from the recovery room.

At 3:00 P.M. Lynn groggily walked back to the van, and then we rode over the cobblestone streets of Guanajuato once more. Carefully Tim helped her walk up the two flights of stairs while I carried Sonya, who was barely eight hours old.

Sixteen incredible hours later, I crawled under the fresh sheets of the hide-a-bed. Our brand-new Sunny was sleeping soundly in her crib. Eric was sprawled on his bed, his blond hair damp on the pillow. Lynn and Tim, heroes of the twentieth century from my viewpoint, were talking quietly in their room.

I smiled into the darkness. Within me a great chorus was singing, "The Lord has done great things for us and we are filled with joy" (Psalm 123:3). The music continued majestically, "From birth I have relied on you; you brought me forth from my mother's womb. I will ever praise you" (Psalm 71:6).

My heart was
     filled
        with
           joy . . .
               praise . . .
                   thanksgiving.

***

We are called to *rejoice in mankind*, and often people do bring us immense joy. We praise God for what He does in and through and to them, and it is right that we should do so.

Paul rejoiced in the event of the proclamation of the gospel, in the faith of the Philippians and in their unity and love (Philippians 1:3,18,25; 2:2). He was excited when a person was received by fellow believers with joy (2:29). He considered his brothers his "joy and crown" (4:1). (And if ever he had seen his granddaughter born, I'm sure he would have rejoiced in that, too!)

But is seeing God operate in the lives of those we love the only way we can be filled with praise? Of course not.

One definition of praise is "occupying your heart with God." But it encompasses even more than that. Webster's defines praise as "an *expression* of approval: commendation."

Praise, then, goes beyond the feeling to an expression of the heart. Joy can be inward. To me, praise is the outward expression of a joyful, inward worship of God.

Three times in Philippians, Paul says we are to rejoice *in the Lord* (3:1, 4:4, 4:10). But instead of rejoicing in the Lord or in anything else, we often operate much like Jonah, who was angry when he should have been celebrating (Jonah 4). We grumble when we should grin, murmur when we should marvel, gripe when we should glory.

I shook my head in wonder when I received a note

from an elderly aunt of mine. She is a widow with a mentally ill son, yet she penned these heartening words:

> I cannot pray today, Lord,
> I can't think what to say,
> Although I'm on my knees, Lord,
> You seem so far away.
>
> The changes in this world, Lord,
> Are more than I can take—
> Loneliness, illness, grief and pain,
> I sometimes think I'll break.
>
> Then a small voice whispers,
> "Forget yourself, and smile,
> Be thankful for your blessings
> On all life's weary miles."
>
> A ray of light is dawning,
> I know You're always near;
> Strength for the day You've promised,
> Your voice is very clear.
>
> "God is our refuge" always,
> We need not walk alone,
> Just help me to remember
> Until life's race is won.[1]

Though discouraged, my aunt was consciously praising God in this verse. Her pain was refined into praise, for *God* was her refuge.

Many reasons to praise God are found in the Scriptures. If nothing else is right in our worlds, we can always stop and praise God for how He made us. "I praise you because I am fearfully and wonderfully made; your works are wonderful, I know that full well" (Psalm 139:14).

I was awed as I read about how we pass on our characteristics to our children:

> The secret to membership lies locked away inside each cell nucleus, chemically coiled in a strand of DNA. Once the egg and sperm share their inheritance, the DNA chemical ladder splits down the center of every gene much as the teeth of a zipper pull apart. DNA re-forms itself each time the cell divides: 2, 4, 8, 16, 32 cells, each with the identical DNA. Along the way cells specialize, but each carries the entire instruction book of one hundred thousand genes. DNA is estimated to contain instructions that, if written out, would fill a *thousand six-hundred-page books.* A nerve cell may operate according to instructions from volume four and a kidney cell from volume twenty-five, but both carry the whole compendium. It provides each cell's sealed credential of membership in the body. Every cell possesses a genetic code so complete that the entire body could be reassembled from information in any one of the body's cells.[2]

Does that blow your mind as it did mine? God is worthy of our praise. "Great is the Lord, and most worthy of praise," David exclaims (Psalm 48:1).

We are to praise God continually and forever for His power, His love, His righteous laws, His wonders, His salvation, His deliverance.[3] Our praise should flow so freely that it could fill thousands of books.

***

Most of us know that we *should* fully praise God. But our question is *how.* The Bible once again gives us the answer.

Did you ever get up on a really gloomy day feeling even more gloomy than the day itself? You knew that you had a choice—to let yourself have a black and blue mood or to praise God for the day He created. So what did you do? You began to sing!

Now I don't sing solos in public. Ever. But I do sing a lot in my home—slightly off-key, but enthusiastically. I deliberately sing songs of praise, for that is exactly what God says to do. "Praise the Lord. How good it is to sing praises to our God, how pleasant and fitting to praise him!" (Psalm 147:1). So I "sing to the Lord a new song, his praise from the ends of the earth" (Isaiah 42:10), and as I sing, my gloomy mood changes.

I have *chosen* to praise, and so my decision to praise and my action of praise change my feelings to ones of praise. It almost always works that way. Did you notice I said *almost*? God even uses the exceptions to teach us another step in the process. For we are to praise whether we start *feeling* like it or not.

I love Psalm 42:11, which says, "But O my soul, don't be discouraged. Don't be upset. Expect God to act! For I know that I shall again have plenty of reason to praise him for all that he will do. He is my help! He is my God!" (*The Living Bible*). And 43:5 continues, "O my soul, why be so gloomy and discouraged? Trust in God! I shall again praise him for his wondrous help; he will make me smile again, *for he is my God!*"

I can *sing* even when my feelings are sorrowful. I can *quote praise verses* even when I don't feel like praising. I can *look to the future* when my days are awash with the present.

I *can*—if I *will*.

Another way of being filled with praise is by *doing deliberate acts of praise*. We can *give to others*, which is an act of praise to God (Hebrews 13:15-16, 2 Corinthians 9:13). We can even *dance* before the Lord, which was a common form of acting out praise in Old Testament times

(Psalm 149:3). Have you done that lately? I have a friend who feels praise for the Lord as she does her aerobics to a praise record. She says it makes her feel good on the outside *and* the inside!

Another way to have a heart of praise is to *recount the goodness of God*. Recently at a prayer-and-share luncheon for my support-group Bible study, we began to recount God's goodness. One person recounted praying for a kitten nine years ago, only one of a litter of ten to survive birth. This kitten had been pronounced virtually dead, at least the vet had said it couldn't live through the night and suggested leaving it with him for burial. My friend, a new Christian at the time, decided God was interested in pets, too, so she wouldn't abandon the kitten but brought it home and prayed for its recovery. That cat is *still* a favored member of the family.

Another woman, whose husband was terminally ill with brain cancer, didn't have a job or enough money to go with her husband for specialized surgery in Boston. Discouraged, she walked into a friend's office—who was not a Christian—to see if he had any work for her in her field.

"Yes," he said. "I do have work, but you have to leave for the job on Saturday."

"I can't leave Saturday," she replied. "My husband is ill and has to have surgery."

"You must leave Saturday," he insisted. "I have an immediate job for you—in Boston."

She ended up being able to be with her husband the entire duration of his hospitalization, all expenses paid. She was able to work on her job at her convenience, and, to top it off, she got to stay at the Hilton.

Delighted and full of praise? You bet. I agree with Paul when he said, "How can we thank God enough for you in return for all the joy we have in the presence of our God because of you?" (1 Thessalonians 3:9). Praise will fill our hearts as we recount the goodness of God.

The people of Israel used to praise God by *reading aloud from the Psalms,* a good practice when you are discouraged (2 Chronicles 29:30).

Deliberately telling others about what God has done for you is a very practical form of praise (Psalms 22:22, 52:9, 9:1-2).

Finally, we need to be aware that *praise is a sacrifice to God.* "Through Jesus, therefore, let us continually offer to God a sacrifice of praise—the fruit of lips that confess his name" (Hebrews 13:15).

I recall one time mulling over this verse, wondering how praise is a "sacrifice." The very next day some things happened that put me in a very bad mood, one that I definitely wanted others to be aware of. This verse flashed into my mind. If I was going to "offer the sacrifice of praise to God continually," I was going to have to give up my black mood. To sacrifice it. I was going to have to turn in my "poor me" union card. At times like this, praise is a sacrifice because grumbling and praising are not compatible. Thus we must sacrifice our grumbling.

We are to be perpetually *filled* with praise. The psalmist David said, "My mouth is filled with your praise, declaring your splendor all day long" (Psalm 71:8). Here he was speaking prophetically of Christ, the One who lives in us. As He fills us, we will be filled with praise.

We are not only to be filled, friends: we are to overflow! Psalm 119:171-172 declares, "May my lips overflow with praise, for you teach me your decrees. May my tongue sing of your word, for all your commands are righteous."

Filled and overflowing. May God grant each of us the ability to praise Him continually and forever.

Even if you never get to see your granddaughter born!

NOTES: 1. Poem by Jeanne Kamp.
2. Paul Brand and Philip Yancey, *Fearfully and Wonderfully Made* (Grand Rapids: Zondervan, 1980), pages 45-46.
3. Psalms 30:12, 21:13, 63:3, 119:164, Deuteronomy 10:20-21, Psalms 9:14, 40:1-3.

APPLICATION BIBLE STUDY

1. Name ten things for which you can begin praising God today.

2. What forms of praise do you practice right now? What other forms should you begin using? (For instance, do you sing songs of praise around the house? Do you praise even when you don't feel like it?)

3. According to Psalm 40:2-3 and Jeremiah 17:14, what are some results of praise in a Christian's life?

4. Read aloud as a prayer of praise 1 Chronicles 29:10-13. Think about each attribute of God in these verses, and ask God to teach you daily more and more about how to truly praise Him.

5. Write out Hebrews 13:15 in your own words. What do you think a "sacrifice to God" is? Memorize this verse in your favorite version.

ADDITIONAL STUDY

Look at the following verses, and observe some of the things for which we should praise God. Why should we praise Him for each of these?

(a) Psalm 7:17
(b) Psalm 21:13
(c) Psalm 63:3
(d) Psalm 71:6
(e) Psalm 119:164
(f) Psalm 139:14
(g) Ephesians 1:5-6

7
Full of Laughter

W<small>E HAVE ADDED</small> SO many negative words to our vocabulary these days that it is a wonder we are able to function at all. Words such as *uptight, mid-life crisis*, and *burnout* spatter our conversations. Even much of our humor is based on the negative—a brand of sarcasm that puts down other people. Because the "sitcoms" on TV are full of such tragicomedy, we unconsciously emulate them, filling our lives with the wrong kind of qualities.

I'm not saying all such humor is wrong. But I am saying that I want to develop the trait of laughing *with*, not *at* the expense of, another person.

Somehow as we struggle under great pressures in life,

the ability to laugh purely, unselfconsciously, uproariously, or sometimes to laugh at all, gradually fades.

And yet. . . .

Have you ever watched a small boy going home from school by himself—I mean really *observed* him? If you have, you will never doubt that our God is the Lord of love and laughter.

Once I observed a pudgy child of six or so sploshing home—very slowly. One little foot dragged in half circles, making trails in the light snow. As he stood on the corner waiting for the walk sign, with one mittened finger he brushed each flake of snow meticulously from the pole of the street lamp. From the look of the ice crystals on his jacket, he had already made "angels" in an empty lot and had been in a snowball fight with his friends. Very carefully, he picked one foot up, then pressed it firmly on an unbothered piece of snow. The other was placed at right angles to his first print, for a reason known only to this winter child.

As I was waiting for the light to change, I studied him and started to smile. The smile drifted into a giggle, and the giggle graduated to a full-blown roar. God bless 'um! "Go for it!" I encouraged silently.

On my dreary days, I probably wouldn't have noticed his deliberations. On my ugly ones, I might have frowned. How tragic for me—not to catch the wonder of the rollicking moments God provides in my life. Many of life's small incidents are just plain *fun*—if our perspective is in tune.

We were happily babysitting for our grandchildren on one occasion while their parents took a much needed evening out. Sunny, fourteen months, was already in bed. Eric, age four, was delaying the process as long as possible. A bath, which he enjoyed but knew was a prelude to bed, was in the offing, so he was using every conceivable tactic to stall.

We were all sitting on the back porch enjoying the lovely summer evening. I said, "I know, Eric! Why don't we three take a hot tub and then put you into the bath straight from there?"

Suddenly his elfin face creased in the biggest of smiles. He crossed the porch, patted my arm like an ancient bene- factor, and beamed, "Gamma, dat's a *gwate* idea!"

Jack and I burst into laughter, and Eric joined us with- out having an idea what we were laughing about. It was enough for him that we were enjoying each other.

My mother would always chuckle as she related this humorous incident that took place when I was three: I was apprehensive about sleeping in a dark room, so I did everything possible to delay bedtime and keep her in the room with me. Finally Mother said, "You aren't alone here, Carole. Jesus is with you."

After a pause I replied, "Mommy, do you love Jesus?"

"Of course, dear," was the answer.

"Then why don't you stay up here where Jesus is?"

One of the ways that Job's friends "comforted" him — and maybe they really *did* with this bit — was in promising that his trials would come to an end and that then "[God] will yet fill your mouth with laughter and your lips with shouts of joy" (Job 8:21).

Filled with laughter! Our God has given us the gift of laughter, and He is greatly pleased if and when we are filled with it.

Often we think of great saints and preachers as sour, proper, humorless, and somber. But Charles Spurgeon is a perfect example of a man of God who loved life and laughter. Frequently he would lean back in the pulpit and *roar* aloud over something that struck him funny. "He infected people with cheer germs. Those who caught the disease found their load lighter and their Christianity brighter."[1]

"Cheer germs"—I like that. May we always be infectious!

If we are alert, we find humor everywhere. Humorous situations surround us. Recently I read of such a situation: "Attending church in Kentucky, we watched an especially verbal and boisterous child being hurried out, slung under his irate father's arm. No one in the congregation so much as raised an eyebrow—until the child captured everyone's attention by crying out in a charming Southern accent, 'Ya'll pray for me now!'"[2]

I suppose children provide one of the primary sources for laughter. Their imaginations and ways of expressing themselves are incredible.

As Jack was waiting in a tedious line to redeem a layaway purchase at a department store, I sat down next to a small, precocious boy—about four—and we began to talk. When he went to get a drink, I asked him where the water went.

He pointed to his mouth and said, "In there."

"In your mouth?" I queried.

Half laughing, he said, "No. No."

"In your neck?"

"Oh, *no*."

"In your esophagus?" I pursued.

"No!" he laughed loudly. "A 'sophagus' is a spider animal."

"Oh? What does a 'sophagus' look like?"

His eyes widened with delight. "It don't have no head. Only furry legs. No tail. And it flies, but it got no wings."

And off he went into the most imaginative and delightful description of a sophagus you ever heard. Gone were my doldrums and impatience at having to wait in an uncomfortable chair. I came away with enough stored-up spasms of mirth for the rest of the evening. I can still see that shining-eyed, earnest little boy saying, "*No*! A sophagus is a spider animal."

But how do we work on being *filled* with laughter? Are there things we can actually do to work on developing the gift of humor that lies within us (*very* deep in some cases)?

Yes, I believe there are some things we can do to help ourselves—and others—learn to laugh.

First of all, *we can actively look for things to laugh at and about.* Consider the story of a very uptight man who had been diagnosed as having an incurable disease. As he studied the nature of his illness, he realized that it might have been caused by stress due to his high-strung temperament. Consequently he decided that laughing would be stress-reducing and therapeutic. His goal was to laugh at least two hours each day, so he rented old Laurel and Hardy films and played them by the hour. He read humorous books. Gradually this man learned to laugh. And he recovered.

You might be skeptical of this story, but remember the verse in Proverbs that says, "A merry heart is good medicine" (17:22).

One of the great joys of traveling to Australia a few years ago was observing the delightful sense of humor the Aussies have. They never seemed to mind that we got such a charge out of their expressions of speech. When I would look startled and say, "What does *that* mean?" they would grin, tell me what it meant, and then go on to a few other amusing expressions.

Do you know what "a real bonzer sheila" is? A "chock-a-block"? "Airy-fairy"? How about "boil a billy"?

Well, a bonzer sheila is a real good sort, a chock-a-block means it's "full up," airy-fairy means it doesn't make much sense, and to boil a billy means to have a cup of tea. Some of the others, such as "much of a muchness" (too similiar) and "he did his block" (lost his temper) you might figure out without asking.

Language throughout our own country is comical. The first time we heard a Texan say he was going to "carry his girl" someplace, we thought, "Poor thing! She must be a cripple." It took us several times before we figured out he was just *taking* her somewhere.

We often take life, as well as ourselves, all too seriously. We should keep reminding ourselves, "Happy is the person who can laugh at himself. He will never cease to be amused."[3]

It was January and I had flown home to Colorado the day of the worst storm of the year. I was traveling alone, and I had encountered delays on every lap of the trip. The final blow came as we were sitting on the plane in Denver at 11:00 P.M. waiting for a mechanical problem to be fixed.

"We are sorry, ladies and gentlemen," the stewardess said so sweetly that she didn't sound as if she really had any regrets at all. "We've just been informed that the Colorado Springs airport is closed because of fog. If you will all deplane and go to our agent, he will assist you."

Mass confusion. Impossible lines. No luggage coming off the belt. Being blown by gale-force winds and snow while waiting for the motel limousine. Seven degrees below zero.

Finally at 12:30 A.M., I stood shivering in a chilly, depressing motel room, brushing my teeth with an impossibly hard toothbrush from the airline kit I'd been given in lieu of my luggage.

"I don't *believe* this trip," I thought grimly. A story came to mind of a flight during which a voice came over the intercom: "Ladies and gentlemen, may I have your attention, please? You are on an experimental flight. Everything on this aircraft is automatic, run by computers and instruments. You have no pilot or crew. But there is no cause to worry. Everything has been thoroughly checked and *nothing* can possibly go wrong . . . go wrong . . . go wrong . . . go wrong."

I murmured under my breath, "That's right. Nothing more can possibly go wrong . . . go wrong . . . go wrong."

With no luggage, I was without robe, slippers, makeup, or change of clothes. I reached into the airline emergency kit and brightened. "O great," I thought. "They have given me a chapstick" (Colorado is extremely dry, so a lot of lotion is required to avoid cracking lips.) I took out the small round container, twisted it up, and liberally applied it.

"Strange consistency," I thought, and, putting on my glasses, I began to laugh. I had just thoroughly deodorized my lips. "Well, now my lips won't sweat!"

How do we learn to laugh at ourselves?

As people and especially as parents we need to pray for wisdom about this one. I remember times as a child when I was nervous to the point of being sick whenever I had to play in a piano recital. (I hated them!) One time Mother lightened the situation by saying, "Tell you what, Carole. As you walk up on the stage of the school auditorium, why don't you trip and fall flat? That will relax *everyone.*" (She knew that parents and children alike were anxious and nervous.)

I never did trip, of course, but the knowledge that she wouldn't take it hard if I *did,* made me able to accept the mistakes I made in my recital piece with grace, if not mirth. She helped me take myself less seriously.

The small boy of a friend of mine accidentally spilled his milk all over his freshly-put-on suit. His eyes got big as he looked up at his mother with lips quivering, tears ready. Although it was quite a spill, he looked so woebegone that his mother started to chuckle. He was absolutely surprised, then delighted as they laughed together. (I suppose this one could backfire on you, but in this instance it was so *right.*)

Perhaps you had a different sort of parent.

After a time of great hilarity in the car with some young people, one girl commented wistfully, "You know, I can't remember a single time when our family laughed together." I ached for her. She had so much to learn about life all by herself in order to compensate for a family that could not laugh.

Humor is an art that can be developed. If you haven't learned to laugh, especially at yourself, find some people who have mastered the art, then cultivate them as friends. Become a student of people: observe them and ask them questions to unravel the threads of learning to laugh.

Memorize Philippians 4:8 — "Fix your thoughts on what is true and good and right. Think about things that are pure and lovely, and dwell on the fine, good things in others. Think about all you can praise God for and be glad about." (*The Living Bible*). Ask God to change your thought life. Stop dwelling on negative things.

Begin today to practice the "no-knock" policy of James Dobson. Refuse to "knock" another person or even yourself. Discipline yourself so that you aren't having negative thoughts, such as, "Stupid me."

Read humorous books, stories, or articles. Practice *laughing out loud.* It may scare you at first, but persevere. Accept yourself in the light of God's total and incredible love and delight for you.

G. K. Chesterton said, "It is really a natural trend to lapse into taking oneself gravely because it is the easiest thing to do . . . for solemnity flows out of men naturally, but laughter is a leap. It is easy to be heavy, hard to be light. Satan fell by force of gravity." (Did you get that little twist there? If not, work on it.)

We need to practice keeping alert to things that we know others would appreciate and chuckle at.

When Eric was two and a half, we bought him a tricycle for Christmas. The week before, Dad Mayhall (who was a whiz at fixing sewing machines and other appliances) and Jack (who is a whiz, period) worked one *long* evening to figure out how to get one small tricycle from a jillion parts into a working vehicle. By the end of the evening, both were fit to be tied (whatever that means—talk about a strange expression!).

So we were especially appreciative when Lynn, our daughter, sent a cartoon in one of her letters. The cartoon depicted a frustrated father kneeling in the midst of a living room cluttered with nuts, bolts, handlebar, wheels, and so on, of an "easy to assemble" tricycle, exclaiming in his frenzy, "HO—HO—HO—HO—HO!" Lynn wrote above the cartoon, "After last Christmas, thought you'd appreciate this!!"

God's gift to us is laughter, but some of us have let the gates of humor get so corroded and rusty that they squeak open with difficulty, if at all. Yet humor is an attribute that can be used to attract people to the Savior.

Isabel Kuhn, in *Second Mile People*, tells of Dorothy, whose special gift was her radiance, "her shining, happy joy in her walk with the Savior." Isabel says she doubted that Dorothy ever knew she possessed this quality. "She thought she should have been preaching, when as a matter of fact the Holy Spirit was using her gift of shining, to the very fullest extent in the life she had prayed to touch."

Isabel quotes the following poem by A.S. Wilson:

Indwelt
Not merely in the words you say,
Not only in your deeds confessed,

But in the most unconscious way
    Is Christ expressed.

Is it a beatific smile,
A holy light upon your brow;
Oh no, I felt His Presence while
    You laughed just now.

For me 'twas not the truth you taught,
To you so clear, to me still dim,
But when you came to me you brought
    A Sense of Him.

And from your eyes He beckons me,
And from your heart His love is shed,
Till I lose sight of you and see
    The Christ instead.[4]

Kitty Muggeridge wrote this about Mother Teresa and her order of nuns: "They are also enjoined to laugh. 'Laughter is a way of communicating joy, and joy is a net of love by which we can catch souls.' This is the spirit in which the nuns trip off smiling to run about the dark, squalid slums, to tend the sick and dying and bathe the maggot-infested sores of emaciated bodies."[5]

O friends, may God teach us to *laugh*—at ourselves and with others. May we see the amusement in the antics of an anteater, be sensitive to the rollicking rhythm of a children's band, be aware of the mirthful moments, the hilarious happenings, and funny fantasies that surround us.

As He did with Job, God will fill *our* mouths with laughter and shouts of joy.

NOTES: 1. Charles Swindoll, *Standing Out: Being Real In an Unreal World* (Portland: Multnomah Press, 1983), page 17.
          2. *Reader's Digest*, April 1980, page 76.

3. From "Quotable Quotes," *Reader's Digest*, July 1980, page 149.
4. Isabel Kuhn, *Second Mile People* (Robesonia, PA: OMF Books).
5. "Mother Teresa of Calcutta," Kitty Muggeridge, *Bright Legacy*, page 11.

APPLICATION BIBLE STUDY

1. (a) When was the last time you remember throwing back your head and roaring with laughter?
   (b) At what do you usually laugh? Sarcasm? Others' humiliation? Others' gaiety? Yourself?
   (c) On a scale from one to ten, rate yourself in your tendency to laugh. Then ask your spouse, your children, or your best friend to rate you.

2. What do you think Job's friend meant when he said, "[God] will yet fill your mouth with laughter and your lips with shouts of joy"? (Job 8:21).

3. (a) Write out Proverbs 17:22 in your own words. Do you have a cheerful heart or crushed spirit? How does one cancel the other?
   (b) Matthew 11:28-30 offers another solution for a downcast spirit. What is it, and how does it relate to the ability to laugh?
   (c) What other ways to be uplifted in spirit have you learned from this book?

4. Write down two things to do this week to develop a cheerful heart. Pray for them every day, and do them!

5. Memorize Proverbs 17:22, and think about it this week every day.

8
Filled with Assurance of Faith

Faith is a willing & deliberate
confidence in God
unquestionable belief in God
complete trust, confidence

I DID A DOUBLE take and read the ad again.

SPECIAL PURCHASE
Authentic, genuine imitation
Gucci-style handbags.
Save 87½%!

The dictionary says that "authentic" refers to something that can be believed or accepted, something trustworthy or reliable.

"Genuine" refers to something that is not counterfeit or artificial.

"Imitation" means an artificial likeness or counterfeit.

Question: How can a handbag be an authentic, genuine imitation? I guess the answer would be by being a trustworthy, reliable, artificial counterfeit.

One cannot have faith in an imitation. Both the faith and the object of that faith must be real. God says we are to "draw near with a *true* heart in full assurance of faith. . . . Let us hold fast the profession of our faith without wavering; for he is faithful that promised. . ." (Hebrews 10:22-23, *King James Version*).

We are to have full assurance. In other words, we are to be *filled* with faith.

I have some questions about that. I guess the one uppermost in my mind is, "Does the ambivalence of my feelings (being scared, worried, or depressed, for instance) indicate I *don't* have the full assurance of faith?

My thoughts travel back. . . .

***

It was a "whiteout." I was driving alone in a shrieking blizzard.

Terrified.

The windshield wipers, beating a steady rhythm against the glass, were useless. The beam from the headlights reflecting off the wall of white only added to my blindness, as masses of snow swirled around my car. Moist chunks of ice froze to the blue metal.

Wearing a white blouse, red wool suit, and high heels, I had left the women's retreat just an hour before to drive the two-hundred and fifty miles home to Colorado Springs. As I left the small campground in western Nebraska, the winds were gusting heavily and a bit of rain struck my windshield, but I anticipated no problem on this early October day, so I hummed happily to a tape of my favorite songs.

Subconsciously, I realized that I had not seen a car on

the road for some time, but I ignored the alarm bell ringing in my mind. As the road on this windswept plain tilted upward, quite suddenly the blizzard engulfed me. The narrow road offered no opportunity to turn around even if I could have seen where the pavement ended and the ditch began.

"*Please* stop the blowing, Father. I can't *see!*" I yelled aloud.

The wind continued unabated.

"*Please* keep me on the road, Lord," I pleaded. And miraculously, He did.

I edged along blindly, not daring to stop. My small car hugged the road, staggering over drifts without complaint. For a moment I caught a glimpse of tire tracks on the white ribbon of road ahead of me. Then just as quickly they were obliterated by drifts and the falling blasts of furious snow.

Abruptly, I came up behind a pickup truck. A man, leaning into the wind and snow, moved in slow motion to my car. He said, "Wait a moment. Then follow that truck. There is a big drift ahead. He'll try to break a path through for you."

But in the one moment that I delayed, the truck's taillights disappeared completely and I was unable to tell where or if he had made it through. Sightless, I crept ahead, praying every minute.

My blue Omega, plastered white, trudged slowly upward. At last I was at the top of the plateau. A small truck blocked the road, so I came to a stop with no place to go. As the wind died down momentarily, I could make out other vehicles—snowplows, trucks, other cars—many of them half-buried, resting at crazy angles in ditches.

I sat numb, with a calm not mine overriding my terror.

Finally a man from the highway department struggled

over to my car. As I rolled down my window, a blast of wind and cold air blew in with his voice. "You'd better pull in to that church lot," he yelled. "It's warm in the church and other people are there. You will have to wait for a snowplow, and then we will try to caravan you all out of here."

Cautiously, with his help, I backed up and pulled in close to the chapel. As I entered, a noisy hubbub of voices met me. One family of six, going to a football game that morning, had been sheltered in the church since 8:30 A.M. I glanced at my watch to see that the hands were hovering at 5:00 P.M.

For the next hour we waited, interrupted by the crackling walkie-talkie radios monitoring our plight. "We have two plows stuck here. Need a third," pleaded someone. Then came the answer, "We don't have any more. You're on your own."

A trucker asked me what direction I had come from. When I told him I had driven in from the north, his eyes widened and he said, "*How* did you get through to here?" I thought, "I had *Help!*" but I didn't try to explain. I was the only person who had come from the north in several hours. (No wonder I hadn't seen any cars!) No one else was getting through from that direction.

Two truckers, their rigs almost eclipsing the small church, needed a ride to town. One had decided to desert his truck temporarily after he had almost overturned his rig by braking suddenly for a car that was stuck sideways on the road. He couldn't see the car until he was almost on top of it.

About 5:45 P.M. a plow arrived and the younger trucker agreed to drive my car in the motley caravan. However, if there *was* a plow up front somewhere, it wasn't doing its job, for our convoy of cars and trucks crested drifts and lost the trail many times. The pick-up truck in front of us started to slide. For several moments the driver fought for control, then lost to the ditch on the side. By the time we had offered the occupants a ride (which they declined, deciding to wait for the last truck in our line), the tail-lights of the caravan had disappeared into the blizzard. We were the first car in the rest of the pack.

The older man in the rear seat kept his window cracked to try to see the left side of the road. I watched to the right. Only a giant blank was ahead.

It was the longest thirty minutes of my life, catching up with that caravan, which was waiting for us at a slightly protected spot in the road.

Kimball, Nebraska! At last! I praised God in my heart. As I was letting the truckers out at a place from which they could telephone, I looked for a motel. But all of them seemed to have "No Vacancy" signs in front. Of course. Everyone was in the same fix I was in.

I finally pulled into the sheltering overhang of one of them anyway, and the kindly proprietor let me use his phone to call the chairman of the retreat I had just attended. I asked her if she knew anyone in Kimball who would put me up for the night. The answer was yes.

The lady who took me in was very gracious. She had no electricity at the moment, but she offered a warm home, a hot supper, a soft bed. Gifts from God, through the kindness of His saints.

Driving home the next day—a day later than originally planned, on a roundabout road that was not closed to traffic—I reflected on the ways of God. He could have changed my route to begin with (I usually fly, but decided it was quicker, in this case, to drive). He could have stopped the wind from blowing, or held back the entire storm. But instead of delivering me from the storm, He delivered me *through* the storm. He showed me His love by providing many "good Samaritans," by keeping me on a road I could not see, by guiding that Omega steadily through drifts and barriers, by calming my heart even while I was terrified. (Yes, believe it or not, a part of me remained calm the whole time.)

Through the storm. There are many times God delivers us *from* the storms of life—times we are not even aware of . . . so we never thank Him. But *through* the storm—Ah! Therein lies the knowledge of what God has done! Therein lies praise to Him and the lessons He can teach us.

Our questions about faith swirl around us, dropping like giant snowflakes on the windshield of our minds, sometimes blinding us to the joy of God that comes through the storms. One cries, "Can we be calm and terrified at the same time and call that faith?"

Yes, we can. In considering this question, I began to see the depth of Paul's statement in 2 Corinthians 6:10, where he speaks of being sorrowful, "yet always rejoicing." Friends, it *is* possible—yes, even *probable*, and certainly normal—to have totally different emotions at the same time. God understands.

The writer of the Seventy-third Psalm accurately describes his feelings. He is obviously upset with the success of the wicked around him. To him they are carefree, increasing in wealth, healthy, and free from the burdens of the common man. He even laments his dedication to keep pure: "Surely in vain have I kept my heart pure; in vain have I washed my hands in innocence" (verse 13).

His wisdom keeps him from venting his feelings to others, but he says it *all* to God. He confesses that it is oppressive even to *try* to understand the success of evil men (verse 16).

Then comes the turning point—the key to accepting

and understanding the seeming success of evil people. In verse 17 he says that he did not understand "till I entered the sanctuary of God; *then* I understood their final destiny." When he entered God's presence, he received God's view of the situation.

The only place from which we will be able to glimpse life from God's perspective and have real joy in the midst of a cruel and unjust state of affairs is in God's presence. The psalmist at last perceives the final judgment, and he recognizes God's good plan and reality in his life. "Yet I am always with you; you hold me by my right hand. You guide me with your counsel, and afterward you will take me into glory" (verses 23-24).

The climactic statement comes in verse 25: "Whom have I in heaven but you? And being with you, I desire nothing on earth." But in the very same breath, he admits confusion and contradiction of emotions. "My flesh and my heart may fail, but God is the strength of my heart and my portion forever" (verse 26).

I am glad God includes such passages in His word. He tells me it is OK—normal, good, fine, natural—to feel several emotions at once. In Psalm Seventy-three we see grief, confusion, despair, and discouragement side by side with trust, hope, confidence, security, and, above all, *faith*. I relax when I know that an understanding Creator-Father smiles at the simultaneous diversity of my emotions.

But another serious question blankets the landscape: Is it possible (even OK) to be *concerned* without being worried or anxious? Or is "concern" just another word for anxiety, and therefore sin?

I have to admit that as soon as I got to the home in Kimball, Nebraska, I called Jack so that he *wouldn't* be concerned. (He wasn't—Colorado Springs was absolutely clear!) But my point is that I *expected* Jack's concern for me, and would have been hurt if, after I had been late, he hadn't expressed concern. Is this the same as worry?

Paul says in Philippians 4:6-7, "Do not be anxious [worried] about anything, but in everything, by prayer and petition, with thanksgiving, present your requests to God. And the peace of God, which transcends all understanding, will guard your hearts and your minds in Christ Jesus."

Yet Paul himself says in 2 Corinthians 11:28-29, "Besides everything else, I face daily the pressure of my concern for all the churches. Who is weak, and I do not feel weak? Who is led into sin, and I do not inwardly burn?" Paul was concerned for the welfare of other Christians and for those who were in sin.

To have *concern* means "to have a relation to or bearing on; . . . to draw in; engage or involve." Only the tertiary meaning is "to cause to feel uneasy or anxious." A synonym for concern is *care*.[1]

To *worry* means "to feel distressed in the mind; be anxious, troubled, or uneasy."

The word *worry* comes from an Old English verb, *wyrgan*, which means to strangle or injure, with the sense of choking or tearing at the throat with the teeth.[2] We still use the word in this original meaning when we speak of a cat *worrying* a mouse.

The opposite of worry is "to comfort, solace, soothe, calm."[3] But the opposite of concern is indifference, disregard, carelessness.

We don't want to be indifferent. We do want to be calm. Therefore we must be concerned, but not worried.

Therefore, the answer to my question is, Yes, I can and should be concerned, with a godly concern for the welfare of others. *But* I must cast my *worries* on God. 1 Peter 5:7 says, "You can throw the whole weight of your anxieties upon him, for you are his personal *concern*" (*Phillips*).

God is not *worried* about us—but He is *concerned* about us! Isn't that great?

Perhaps a warning is needed here, however, for we may use the word *concern* when in reality we are worried, fearful, and lacking in trust in God's care and love. Paul was concerned for *people*, not situations. We usually worry about situations, sometimes combining them with people. We worry about the loss of a job, ill health, ill treatment, lack of money, missing planes, losing things—all wrong to do. We are right to be concerned for an alcoholic husband, a hurting friend, a sick child. But it is real cause for celebration to know that God will relieve us of our worries and also share our concerns.

***

I learned a great deal from that snowstorm. I came to understand that although sometimes I have a great diversity of feelings inside, that does not necessarily indicate a lack of faith. But as I mature, my mind and will should grow more and more compatible with my heart and emotions. I still have a great deal of growing and learning to do concerning drawing near to God with "true heart in *full* assurance of faith" (Hebrews 10:22). *The Amplified Bible* calls this the "unqualified assurance and absolute conviction engendered by faith."

We know that "faith is being sure of what we hope for and certain of what we do not see" (Hebrews 11:1). Faith is our confidence when we stand on the Rock, Christ Jesus. John Greenleaf Whittier described such confidence:

> Nothing before, nothing behind;
> The steps of faith
> Fall on the seeming void and find
> The rock beneath.

And then come a trilogy of questions, running something like this: *How can I get more faith? Are some answers to prayer blocked by my lack of faith? What produces faith?* Good, honest questions. Ones that have to be prayed over and investigated.

Once while I was mulling over my puny little faith, God led me to Matthew 14:22-33—the story of Christ walking on the water. I carefully noted the reaction of the disciples, especially the response of Peter.

When the disciples, who were in a boat on the Sea of Galilee, saw Christ walking on the water, they were all terrified—a natural first reaction to the situation.

Christ didn't give them "lecture number one on worry." Instead, He reassured them.

Good old impetuous Peter then showed a tiny grain of faith by saying, "If (and there was still a good big *if* there) it's you, tell me to come to you on the water."

The Lord said, "Come." So Peter got out of the boat and walked on the water toward Jesus. Peter didn't have a great deal of faith, but as a result of his *little* faith, he was willing to put himself in a precarious situation. None of the other disciples did that.

But then Peter felt the fierce wind and looked at the towering water. Just as his doubts were growing as high as the waves, he started to sink. His cry for help reverberated over the sea, "Lord, save me!"

Lecture number two coming up? Of course not. *Immediately* Christ reached out His hand and pulled him up.

It was only then that the deserved rebuke came: "You of little faith, why did you doubt?"

Not even lecture number one. Just a one-sentence reminder.

The response of the disciples, as the Lord and Peter climbed together into the boat and the wind ceased, was to worship. They said, "Truly you are the Son of God."

Peter had just a little faith, but he acted on that belief. It is not our great faith but a little faith *in action* that demonstrates to us God's faithfulness. Who do you think developed more faith in Christ from this incident: Peter or the disciples who stayed in the boat? Of course—it was Peter. It was *he* who walked on the water. And when he began to sink, Christ didn't say, "Too bad, fellow. You should have believed more." No, Christ saved him!

Peter learned the lesson best. He discovered that when trouble comes, even though caused by doubt, Christ never fails when we ask for His help. Peter learned that it is not our great faith but our great *God* who delivers.

Faith grows by knowing and experiencing a faithful God. We get to know Him by beholding Him through His word, and we experience Him by using the little faith we have to step out on His promises. It's been written,

> Whoso draws nigh to God one step
> though doubting dim,
> God will advance a mile
> in blazing light to him.

We have a Father who *cares* and has given us His Holy Spirit to be our Teacher and Guide. If we are open to Him, He is going to alert us when we *worry* about our trouble instead of *trusting* Him. He will assure us that our diversity of feelings in many situations shows not a lack of faith, but our own humanity. The Holy Spirit will help us develop the strong, sure faith that comes from knowing a faithful God, until eventually we will be filled with the full assurance of faith.

Even in a blizzard.

NOTES: 1. *Webster's New World Dictionary* (New York: The World Publishing
            Company, 1970), page 293.
         2. *Webster's New World Dictionary*, page 1639.
         3. From *Reader's Digest Family Word Finder*.

APPLICATION BIBLE STUDY

1. Define the words *faith*, *faithfulness*, and *faithful*.
   (Use a dictionary.)

2. The Bible shows us that we are to have faith in God
   and to be faithful to Him and to His people. According to
   these verses, what are some ways we are to be faithful?
   (a) Proverbs 11:13
   (b) Proverbs 14:5
   (c) Proverbs 25:13
   (d) Proverbs 27:6
   (e) Matthew 24:45-46
       (What is the "household" and the "food"?)
   (f) Luke 16:10
   (g) Luke 16:12
   (h) 1 Corinthians 4:2

3. Look up Hebrews 10:22-23 in at least two translations,
   and then write it out in your own words. How can we
   have "full assurance of faith"?

4. What are you doing to develop your faith? What do you
   feel God would have you do?

5. Memorize one of the verses from this chapter that has
   spoken to you in a special way.

6. What are some rewards of being faithful, according to
   Psalm 31:23, Psalm 101:6, and Proverbs 28:20?

7. Study the life of one of the faithful people in the Bible:
   Abraham, Moses, Ruth, Samuel, David, and Jesus
   are some examples.

9
Filled with Peace

peace of God 5:1+2
peace with God
Ep. 2:13+14

I WAS DASHING up the steps of our administrative office when one of the women working at a nearby desk motioned for me. She was smiling as she said, "I must tell you what my little five-year-old girl said last night. We were singing 'When We Walk with the Lord.' Suddenly I realized that, instead of singing, 'He abides with us still,' she was singing, 'He provides us with still.'"

God does exactly that. He provides me with *still* . . . with peace . . . with quiet. He leads me beside still waters. He restores my soul.

Romans 15:13 says, "May the God of hope *fill* you with all joy and *peace* as you trust in him, so that you may overflow with hope by the power of the Holy Spirit." We are to be filled with joy . . . filled with peace . . . so that we may overflow with hope. Qualities that all of us long for. But how can I be filled with peace? What sort of things prevent me from having peace permeate every corner of my life?

When Paul wrote to the Romans, he said that he would *pray* for joy and peace in their lives. I wonder how many times in the last month you and I have prayed for peace—to be filled with peace as we trust in Him. How often do we pray this for others?

We *must* pray—because we all need God's help.

After taking Jack to the airport rather early in the morning, I braked before turning right on a road that skirts the city. A woman in an old VW paused in front of me, looked to the left (no cars in sight) and then started her right turn. I also glanced to the left (still no cars in sight) and then put my foot on the gas. Looking forward again, I was horrified to discover that the driver in front of me had stopped once more to look to the left. I slammed on my brakes, but it was too late—I rear-ended her small car.

We both got out, shaken but unhurt. Our cars had likewise suffered only minor damage. This stooped, elderly woman immediately began to justify her second stop, saying that she didn't drive much, but that her husband was sick and couldn't drive. I assured her that she had a right to stop as many times on a right turn as she felt necessary and that it was my fault for not being more careful.

But there we stood out in the middle of large fields without a house or store for blocks. I didn't know what the procedure was in this situation—whether to call the police or not.

Suddenly a voice came—seemingly out of the sky. It

was hollow-sounding, distinct, loud. This disembodied voice said, *"Do you need help?"*

Startled, I glanced around. A police car had pulled up about a half-block away and the policeman was using his bullhorn to ask if we needed assistance. I had to laugh out loud as I gestured for him to come.

I needed help from that policeman. And, in a similar way, I need help from God in every area of my life—help that He has promised to give. He extends to us the promise of Isaiah 26:3: "You will keep in perfect peace him whose mind is steadfast, because he trusts in you." A few verses later, Isaiah says, "Lord, you establish peace for us; all that we have accomplished you have done for us" (verse 12).

God is constantly asking, *"Do you need help?"* My answer is always, "Yes. *Please!*"

Our peace *with* God must come before our peace *in* God, however. Isaiah thunders that there is no peace for the wicked (57:21) and that every one of us stands condemned before God. But the good news is that "since we have been justified through faith, we have peace with God through our Lord Jesus Christ, through whom we have gained access by faith into this grace in which we now stand. And we rejoice in the hope of the glory of God" (Romans 5:1-2). The fact that Christ alone has made our peace with God couldn't be more clearly stated than in Ephesians 2:13-14: "But now in Christ Jesus you who once were far away have been brought near through the blood of Christ. For he himself is our peace, who has made the two [Gentile and Jew] one and has destroyed the barrier, the dividing wall of hostility."

Christ-ones have peace with God.

But not all Christ-ones have the peace of God referred to in Philippians 4:6-7: "Do not be anxious about anything, but in everything, by prayer and petition, with thanksgiving, present your requests to God. And the peace *of* God, which transcends all understanding, will guard your hearts and your minds in Christ Jesus." Most of us find this peace that *transcends all understanding* to be a sometimes state. It fades in and out at whim of mood, circumstance, and time of day.

Peace is a state of tranquility, quiet, or security . . . freedom from disquieting or oppressive thoughts or emotions . . . harmony in personal relations. It is completeness, oneness, calmness. The opposite of peace is frustration, conflict, hostility.

I have a dear friend who is going through deep valleys in her life right now. Life to her is patterned in wrinkles, which she is determined to iron out. Her goal reminds me of a beautiful saying someone recently handed me:

> My goal
> is
> God Himself . . .
> at any cost,
> dear Lord,
> by
> any road.

My friend is contending with the issue most of us grapple with frequently. She has been hurt innumerable times by her husband, and she struggles with forgiveness. She is steadily winning that battle.

If part of peace is "harmony in personal relations"— and it is—then forgiveness is not an option for us. Forgiveness is an imperative command.

We will never have God's peace without forgiving people who have hurt or misused us. Never.

We tend to have many false notions about forgiveness. John Hampsch relates a story about such a misconception:

A woman told me that she urged her angry son to "forgive and forget" when another lad stole his candy bar. So he chased the young culprit, beat him to the ground, sat on him and said, "I forgive you for swiping my candy bar, but it would be easier for me to forget if you'd wipe that chocolate off your mouth!"[1]

Which brings us to the statement, "Well, I can forgive, but I certainly will never forget!" Is this possible—forgiving without forgetting?

John Hampsch goes on to say, "Of course one cannot 'forget' having been robbed, raped, embezzled or insulted. Some hurts in life are emblazoned on our memory ineradicably. But hurtful memories, even though they cannot always be removed, must be 'healed' or detoxified. Paul says (1 Corinthians 13:5), 'Love does not hold grudges and will *hardly even notice* when others do it wrong' (*The Living Bible*). . . . To 'forget' such hurts means simply to refuse to mull over them morbidly; it means prayfully to dispel all bitterness from such thoughts when they arise. . . ."

Lack of forgiveness is sin—insidious sin.

I took a walk around our neighborhood this morning and noticed the dark brown stain beginning to spread across my neighbors' lawn. Because they are new to Colorado Springs, they have probably not yet learned how to battle "the fungus." This is a war that is being perpetually waged between my husband and the enemies of a lush lawn. His weapons are fertilizers, weed-killers, and, above all, fungicides. The moment Jack becomes lax in this battle, the brown stain begins to spread.

I thought, "How much like our *spiritual* lives! The moment we 'let up' in the spiritual battle, the brown stain of sin begins taking over our lives."

***

One of the most vital means of having harmony in personal relations—of living in continuous peace—is for us to *work* at peace among our fellow men. "For the kingdom of God is not eating and drinking, but righteousness and peace and joy in the Holy Spirit. . . . So then let us pursue the things which make for peace and the building up of one another. . . . If possible, so far as it depends on you, be at peace with all men. Never take your own revenge, beloved, but leave room for the wrath of God, for it is written, 'Vengeance is Mine, I will repay,' says the Lord" (Romans 14:17, 19; 12:18-19, NASB).

Did you get that? *Never* take your own revenge. Now that is a tough one! In many cultures, the "law of vengeance" is deep and unbending. If someone kills or hurts a member of a family, that family is bound by hundreds of years of tradition to kill or hurt someone in the family that committed the wrong. If the person who did it cannot be found, then revenge may be taken on the other political party, religion, or color. Because of this attitude of vengeance, we have the tragedies of bitter wars in Ireland, Lebanon, and many other countries around the world.

But let's get practical. Most of us don't live in a culture where a strict "law of vengeance" applies. (And even if we did, God's law stands supreme.) But in our hearts, our old nature cries for that vengeance anyway. We've been hurt, and we long to hurt back. We have been smeared, so we lash out to either defend or attack, or maybe even both. Because this avenging tendency is inherent in our very beings, a *supernatural* attitude is needed to keep us from striking back. Such an attitude comes when God's Spirit is in us.

Perhaps you need to take a minute at this point to ask yourself three questions: Am I harboring bitterness against someone for anything at all? Am I trying to reciprocate something negative toward someone who has hurt or insulted me? Am I failing to work toward harmony and peace with my fellow men?

If the answer to any of these questions is yes, please take a few moments to bring that problem to God, asking for His cleansing and healing.

Sin robs us of peace.

***

But what else can I do to be filled with peace?

Years ago, I memorized Psalm 119:165. I am still amazed at its truth every time I recall it: "Great peace have they which love thy law: and nothing shall offend them" (KJV). When I become offended, upset, or hurt, this verse convicts me, telling me that when my heart is centered in God and His word, when my focus is on things above, when I am concentrating on what is "right and true and good," then the petty little happenings of my days cannot have that much effect on me.

Being focused on the word and on the Lord through His word is basic to all the "being filled full's" of Scripture. Romans 8:6 speaks clearly to us: "The mind set on the flesh is death, but the mind set on the Spirit is life and peace" (NASB).

Another building block toward peace is *accepting God's discipline* in our lives. "No discipline seems pleasant at the time, but painful. Later on, however, it produces a harvest of righteousness and peace for those who have been trained by it" (Hebrews 12:11). When we try to run away from, deny, or turn bitter as the result of God's discipline, peace becomes a forgotten factor in our lives. Scripture tells us to "pursue righteousness, faith, love and peace, along with those who call on the Lord out of a pure heart" (2 Timothy 2:22). In purity of life there is peace.

My peace can be "like a river"—wide, deep, and serene

(Isaiah 48:18). It can carry me on to a ripe old age (Proverbs 3:2). Peace is a fruit of the Holy Spirit and part of my inheritance as a believer. But in order to have peace, certain conditions must be met—maintaining a purity of life, working at peace with other people, and keeping my focus on the Prince of Peace. I am to "let peace rule."

The choice is mine.

"Let the peace of Christ rule in your hearts, since as members of one body you were called to peace. And be thankful" (Colossians 3:15).

NOTES: 1. John Hampsch, "Reflections on the Gentle Art of Forgiving," *Logos*, May-June 1981, page 35.

APPLICATION BIBLE STUDY

1. What events caused you anxiety this week? In each instance, try to identify the true cause of your anxiety. (For example, were you anxious because you didn't really believe God was in control, or because you thought God wasn't interested?)

2. Write out John 14:27 in your own words. How do we *let* our hearts be troubled? What can we do to avoid it?

3. Read carefully Philippians 4:6-7, Colossians 3:15, and 1 Peter 5:7. Memorize one of these verses, and write out a sentence describing
   (a) areas of my life in which I am not obeying or practicing this verse.
   (b) one specific instance in which I failed to obey it.
   (c) steps God wants me to take to obey this verse this week. (Things that are always practical to do: (1) put the verse at the top of your prayer list and pray about it every day; (2) keep your verse on your refrigerator or above the sink to review every time you see it; and (3) look for opportunities to practice it and to recite it silently with prayer when you need it.)

10
His Will in Suffering

THE DAY WAS cloudless. The desert sun shimmered as it reflected on slanted rocks and bounced off hard-packed sand. The cacti ranged from giant saguaros, huge arms curving toward heaven, to squat, round, spiny humps clinging to earth.

Jack and I had been silent for many miles, each absorbed in thought as we drove home from Phoenix that April day. But as we entered a small town, I glanced at a sign and laughed, shattering the companionable silence. The sign read:

AZTEC, NEW MEXICO
5,667 friendly people and 6 old soreheads.

Somebody in Aztec has a delightful sense of humor.

My next thought was, "I wonder if the six old sore-heads recognize who they are. Or maybe each of the 5,667 friendly people from time to time thinks he or she is one of those soreheads."

I would.

In *Lord of My Rocking Boat*, I wrote about many of the things that cause us to lose our cool—pressures, pain, people. Lately I've been realizing that a primary factor in understanding and accepting those pressures, trials, and suffering, is our view of the purpose of life.

I have heard it said that "God did not give us a happy spirit to make us happy, but a Holy Spirit to make us holy." Whenever I get squeezed into believing that the purpose of life is to bring delight to *me*, I'm in trouble. God wants to delight me, to be sure. He desires to shower my life with His riches, His treasures, His good things. And that is exactly what He does. But if I consider those "good things" to be plenty of money, gobs of love, unconditional acceptance from other people, and untold happiness throughout my life, then I must have a reading disability.

For Paul says very clearly, "For this reason, since the day we heard about you, we have not stopped praying for you and asking God to fill you with the knowledge of his will through all spiritual wisdom and understanding. And we pray this in order that you may live a life worthy of the Lord" (Colossians 1:9-10).

We as believers are to be filled with the knowledge of God's will. But *how*? Through all spiritual wisdom and understanding. *Why*? So we may live a life worthy of the Lord!

"Filled" means to be complete, satisfied, saturated, occupied to capacity.

"Knowledge" means understanding, enlightenment, discernment, comprehension, acquaintance.

We are called to be *saturated with enlightenment* concerning the will of God—*occupied to capacity* with understanding concerning His desire for our lives.

Our whole age is obsessed with negative thinking. The world lacks true understanding. Its philosophy is one without lasting purpose or hope. Actor and director Alan Alda, speaking to his daughter's graduation class, expressed this sense of relative futility:

> The door is inching a little closer toward the latch and I still haven't said it. Let me dig a little deeper. Life is absurd and meaningless—unless *you* bring meaning to it, unless *you* make something of it. It is up to us to create our own existence.
>
> No matter how loving or loved we are, it eventually occurs to most of us that deep down inside, we're all alone. When the moment comes for you to wrestle with that cold loneliness, which is every person's private monster, I want you to face the damn thing. I want you to see it for what it is and win.
>
> When I was in college, 25 years ago, the philosophy of existentialism was very popular. We all talked about nothingness; but we moved into a world of effort and endeavor. Now no one much talks about nothingness; but the world itself is filled with it.
>
> Whenever that sense of absurdity hits you, I want you to be ready. It will have a hard time getting hold of you if you're already in motion. You can use the skills of your profession and other skills you have learned here, dig into the world and put it into better shape.
>
> (He then talked about clean air, water, putting an end to crime, suffering, etc. Then he concluded his speech.)
>
> There's plenty to keep you busy for the rest of your life. I can't promise this will ever completely reduce that sense of absurdity, but it may get it down to a manageable

level. It will allow you once in a while to bask in the feeling that, all in all, things do seem to be moving forward.[1]

I almost cried when I read this article. I thought, "With all his talent and intellect, is that the only hope he can give to his daughter and her graduation class?" What a contrast to Paul's ringing words of hope—"asking God to fill you with the knowledge of his will through all spiritual wisdom and understanding."

Think of it! God gives us spiritual wisdom and understanding, enabling us to have knowledge of His will. And this knowledge, when we are filled with it, makes our lives worthy of the Lord!

Some factors of His will are that we be holy, joyful, always praying, doing good, obeying God, and being filled with His Spirit.[2] But the one factor we *don't* like to think about, as we bask in the light of His riches and treasures, is that His will for each of us includes *suffering*.

Did you say, "How's that again?" Many books these days proclaim health, wealth, and happiness as the legacy of every Christian. I am convinced that this philosophy is man's dream, not God's plan. Some people have not done their scriptural homework.

The prime purpose of this life is to know God and to be conformed to the image of His Son. When we grasp the deep, vital truth that God achieves His purposes largely through trials and temptations, then we can "welcome them as friends" (James 1:2-5, *Phillips*).

The story is told of a heavyset woman who went to an exercise and diet clinic. The first thing the supervisor did was draw a silhouette on a mirror in the shape she wished to become. As she stood before the mirror, she bulged out over the silhouette. The instructor told her, "Our goal is for you to fit this shape."

For many weeks the woman dieted and exercised. Each week she would stand in front of the mirror, but her volume, while decreasing, still overflowed. And so she exercised harder and dieted more rigidly. Finally one day, to everyone's delight, as she stood in front of the mirror she was conformed to the image of the silhouette.

It takes time and work to be conformed to the image of God's Son. The discipline of sorrow and suffering, the exercise of pain and trials conform us to His image.

A sculptor once fashioned a magnificent lion out of solid stone. When asked how he had accomplished such a wonderful masterpiece, he replied, "It was easy. All I did was to chip away everything that didn't look like a lion."

All God does is chip away everything in our lives that doesn't look like Christ.

Peter states, "Those who suffer *according to God's will* should commit themselves to their faithful Creator and continue to do good" (1 Peter 4:19). Suffering comes in many guises and forms.

Almost every day we experience emotional suffering— perhaps vicariously as a friend sobs out her story, or through a loved one's plight. As we mature, as our world of friends grows larger, as we become older, we can expect this sort of suffering to increase. Elizabeth Rooney says:

I am beginning to learn more about the Cross. I always thought that to walk the way of the Cross meant to seek suffering, and this seemed perverse. I am beginning to realize that it means to learn to love and the more people I love and the more intensely and tenderly I love them, the more opportunities for suffering are presented, as life happens to them and as I learn to share their burdens and care about their cares. Intercession goes well with this because praying for people does make you love them more and more.[3]

But often our own emotions cramp us in spasms, both large and small, as we go about absorbed in our own everyday affairs.

Many of us suffer emotionally because of loneliness and separation. According to researchers, one out of every four Americans suffers from loneliness. Approximately thirteen percent of all married people say they are lonely and not in love.[4]

Separation from loved ones causes deep emotional suffering—whether by distance, death, or rejection.

On Christmas of 1979, I wrote these words:

There must have been a great, aching tug in Your heart, Father, when You said goodbye as Your Son left Your warm home in heaven. You knew what He'd suffer before You would welcome Him home again. You knew the agony and pain He'd bear.

A few months ago a widowed mother flew to San Francisco to say goodbye as her single daughter flew off alone to Indonesia for four years. What a heartache for both mother and daughter.

And now in three days Tim, Lynn, and Eric are to board a plane to leave us. They are a warm, intimate, beloved unit. Jack and I can stand shoulder to shoulder to whisper our farewells.

Yet . . .

The giant ache . . . the tug . . . the tears well up in my heart. That little Eric has wrapped his arms around my heart so tightly that the imprint will never completely leave . . . and I wouldn't want it to. Lynn and Tim, so precious . . . with one part of me I am clapping my hands with thanksgiving and praise that they want to serve You . . . that they are willing to leave friends and family and home to serve You.

With another whole part of me, I weep at their leaving.
So it must have been with You, Lord God.
Only more. Much, much more.

Physical separation causes emotional suffering. Worse
are the feelings of rejection we all experience—rejection
by someone we love through a broken engagement, a
child turning his back on a parent, the excruciating pain
of a divorce.

And then comes the rending and final pain of death,
with its dark, gnawing, unanswered questions. I think
back. . . .

***

Her tear-stained face was a mirror of her troubled heart.

Two weeks before, in what the world would look upon
as a tragic, meaningless accident, her teenage son had skidded
on ice, crashed into a wall, and been thrown out of the car
directly in the path of another vehicle. The truck dragged
him for a half mile before releasing his body in a snow-
covered field. Tragic? Yes. Meaningless? No.

After just two weeks, several of the boy's teenage friends
had received his Savior. Immeasurable grace had lifted
the hearts of parents and family, bringing forth praise and
thanksgiving in their hearts and on their lips. Grace to overcome many of the "whys."

Of course there was weeping. Mourning. Pain. Grief.
But they knew that the pain was on their side, the joy
on their son's.

Still, her concerned face turned toward us and her
voice trembled.

"He was so young," she said. "My one great concern
is, Will he have any trophies for the Master? Or did he
go to heaven empty-handed?"

A deep and probing question. Without answer, really. And yet . . .

I had just been reading the life story of Amy Carmichael. Time after time she spoke of small children dying, reaching out their arms to Jesus as He welcomed them Home. Did *they* go "empty handed"?

Jim Elliot once said, "God is not in the business of peopling heaven just with old people." He died at 29, martyred in Ecuador at the full flush of his ministry. Did he go with fewer "trophies" than if he'd lived to his three-score years and ten? Would that be fair of a just and loving Father?

Two possibilities come to mind:

(1) We each have an allotted time — an assignment of a precise length. It is not the length of life but what I do with the length I have that is the pertinent factor.

(2) God is all-knowing. He knows what Jim Elliot would have done with another forty-plus years of life had it been allotted to him. In His greatness, would God not give Jim the "trophies" he would have won for the Master so that Jim could have the precious privilege of laying them at his Savior's feet?

Would not the God of the universe give to those Indian children, whom He welcomed into His presence at such a young age, the rewards and crowns they would have won had they lived to serve Him to an old age?

There is no Scripture that in black and white answers this question. There are certain secret things that alone belong to God (Deuteronomy 29:29). But we can *know* that our God, who names all the stars in the heavens, does *all things well*.

We should take on the perspective of David, who said, "As for me, my contentment is not in wealth but in seeing you and knowing all is well between us. And when I awake in heaven, I will be fully satisfied, for I will see you face to face" (Psalm 17:15, *The Living Bible*).

Death for us means awakening in heaven and seeing our Lord—face to face. What comfort it is to know that death is not an end but a beginning—to know that we are not in the land of the living going to the land of the dying, but that we are in the land of the dying going to the land of the living.

When the great chemist Sir Michael Faraday was on his deathbed, some journalists questioned him as to his speculations concerning the soul and death. "Speculations!" said the dying man in astonishment. "I know nothing about speculations. I am resting on certainties."

***

Have you ever reflected on the difference between an ordinary trial and a "trial of your faith"? (1 Peter 1:6-7). Such a trial takes place when you cannot see the promises of God operating at the moment. Of course, the promises of God are *always* operating, but sometimes it seems like God is not arriving, or else arriving late. During these times our very souls suffer.

I remember years ago when almost everything in our lives was falling apart. We were broke, friends close to us were critical of us (that is an understatement), we felt that our ministry was a total failure. We were in the ministry because of certain promises from God, but as far as I could see they were not coming to pass. It was a "trial of my faith."

Each morning I cried to God, "Lord, I can't get through this day without You. Help!" And so God's presence filled my heart so that I could survive the day—barely. During that time, I never doubted God's existence or His presence in my life. But I did wonder if He had put us on the shelf, or if we had done something to make Him give up on us. We were seeing no answers to prayer nor were we seeing His promises to us fulfilled.

During that time, a Christian leader who did not know anything about what we were enduring began to talk about trials. He said, "When I finish going through a trial, I want to be able to look back and say, 'I never once doubted God.'"

I was sick inside. I wanted to shout at him, "*Yes*, I'd like to be able to say that, too! But I *am* doubting! Every day I am just barely making it! I am terrified when I think that perhaps God has given up on us."

God taught me some precious lessons through that time—lessons we couldn't have learned any other way. He brought me (a ministry-oriented, people-pleasing person) to the place where I prayed—and meant it, too—"Lord, if You never want me to succeed or have a ministry again in this life, it's *all right*. I know that the first thing you want is *me*, and for me to be conformed to Your image. If my never having any ministry again is the best way for You to accomplish these purposes, *I am willing*."

And then one day we turned the corner from that awful period. God began to fulfill His promises so fast that we couldn't keep up writing them down. It was as if He were saying, "Carole, I love you. I am a faithful God. Your questions and fears will never make Me deny My character. I will be faithful to you even when you question, I will love you when you lack love for Me. I will be true to you when you doubt."

I fell in love with my Father more deeply than ever before. God loves me when I don't even deserve it. He loves me when I am confused and doubting. *He loves me.*

It was a message embedded in silver.

But lessons of gold were waiting.

NOTES: 1. Alan Alda, "Dig Into the World" (commencement speech to his daughter's class), *Reader's Digest*, May 1981, pages 86-87.
2. 1 Thessalonians 4:3, 5:16-18, 1 Peter 2:15, 3:17, Ephesians 1:5-9, 5:15-18.
3. Luci Shaw, "Elizabeth Rooney," *Bright Legacy*, page 118.
4. Carin Rubenstein and Phyllis Shaver, *In Search of Intimacy* (New York: Delacorte, 1982).

APPLICATION BIBLE STUDY

1. Read aloud Colossians 1:9-11. Read it again, putting your own name in it. Pray this for yourself every day for the next week.

2. For each of these verses, write down what it says is God's will for you and the world, and then write how you can conform to that will.
   (a) Ephesians 1:5-10
   (b) 1 Thessalonians 4:3
   (c) 1 Thessalonians 5:16-18
   (d) 1 Peter 2:15
   (e) 1 Peter 3:17

3. Why do you think suffering is a part of God's will for us? See 1 Peter 1:7 and James 1:3-4.

4. Write out 1 Peter 4:19 in your own words.

5. What suffering are you experiencing right now? What are you learning through it?

6. This week ask a godly friend who is suffering in some way what he or she is learning from God through the trial.

11
Filled with Knowledge of His Will

OVER THE TRIPLE doorways of the Cathedral of Milan there are three inscriptions spanning the splendid arches. Over one arch is carved a beautiful wreath of roses, and underneath is the legend, "All that which pleases is but for a moment." Over the other is sculptured a cross, and there are the words, "All that which troubles us is but for a moment." But beneath the great central entrance to the main aisle is the inscription, "That only is important which is eternal."

When we are filled with the knowledge of God's will— actually involved in what we know He wants for us—then we are living for the permanent and the eternal.

My friend Jeanie is suffering. While ministering in Iran, her only brother died of an aneurysm at age thirty-nine. Separated by an ocean from her parents, she is impotent to help her father, who is rapidly failing both mentally and physically. Her mother's strength is daily being depleted in caring for him. Other concerns, deep and hurting, peck away at Jeanie's life. And now she has discovered that she has diabetes.

I've observed Jeanie closely. Daily suffering is making her more like Jesus.

I doubt if Jeanie has it all deciphered and neatly out-lined—one rarely does in the midst of such a furious on-slaught. As I saw her pain, I had the urge to sit down and write to her some of the things God is showing me. I will probably never send the letter—meaningless words when pain fills your cup to the brim—but perhaps one day we'll talk together about lessons God has taught us both. I mentally wrote:

My dear friend,

When I met you yesterday, you smiled in greeting, but I felt your pain hovering just beneath your smile. I ache for you and with you.

The suffering you are experiencing is difficult to accept, let alone understand. But I'm convinced that our suffering is necessary in order to perfect us and make us—both now and in heaven—what God wants us to be. I see it happening in you.

Even secular philosophers, while not understanding the purpose of pain, see its value. One author says, "No one knows why life must be so punishing to some of God's finest creatures. Perhaps it is true that everything has a price and we must sacrifice something precious to gain something else. The poets and philosophers say adversity, sorrow and pain give our lives an added dimension. Those who suffer deeply touch life at every point; they drain the cup to the dregs while others sip only the bubbles on top. Perhaps no man can touch the stars unless he has known the depths of despair—and fought his way back."[1]

"They drain the cup to the dregs." Interesting thought, isn't it? Drinking fully from life's cup of suffering and trials. The poet Elizabeth Rooney says of grief, "It's so important to live fully. Since grief is my assignment for today, Lord, help me grieve wholeheartedly, allowing the reality of the grief to possess me until it becomes appropriate to move beyond it."[2]

It must be that we need these "dark threads" of suffering in our lives in order to be totally *alive*. A poem I have read many times speaks to this truth:

My life is but a weaving
　　Between my Lord and me,
I cannot choose the colors
　　He worketh steadily.

Ofttimes He weaveth sorrow,
　　And I in foolish pride
Forget He sees the upper
　　And I, the underside.

Not till the loom is silent
　　And the shuttles cease to fly
Shall God unroll the canvas
　　And explain the reason why.

The dark threads are as needful
　　In the Weaver's skillful hand
As the threads of gold and silver
　　In the pattern He has planned.[3]

Jeanie, the dark threads planned for you are patterning your life in His steps.

It is *God's* strength that enables you to endure. Corrie ten Boom writes,

> Your strength, my weakness—here they always meet,
> When I lay down my burden at Your feet.
> The things that seem to crush will in the end
> Be seen as rungs on which I did ascend!
>
> Thank You, Lord.[4]

There is nothing, *no thing*, too big for God to handle. He has declared, "My grace is sufficient for you" (2 Corinthians 12:9). I have friends who say, "Carole, you just don't understand. You have never been through a divorce . . . a husband's or child's death . . . total rejection from your family," and the list goes on. They are right. But God's promises are just as true as they have been throughout eternity and His promises are bigger—better—than my experiences. It is God who promises strength in our weakness, comfort in our troubles, compassion for our hurts. I don't have to have personal experience through every circumstance in life to know that His promises *never* fail.

It helps to know and *feel* that God understands all that I am enduring and that He hurts right along with me. Gladys Hunt describes God's empathy quite well:

> God understands about grief. The Son of Man is called "a man of sorrows and acquainted with grief" (Isaiah 53:3). If we understand anything at all about the cross, we know God understands suffering. Our grief, our confusion, our doubts, our anger are safe with Him. We can tell Him all of these—in sobs or in shouts—and He *will* hear us. We may have to wait to hear and see Him in return. We can't

hear when we're screaming and we can't see properly when our eyes are blurred with tears. But He will wait. We determine our capacity to receive from God, but even here He uses time to heal our exhaustion and tenderness to heal our aches until we want Him.[5]

I remember what Dean Denler said while hospitalized with terminal cancer: "Only during my brief stay on earth can I give God the pleasure of praising him in the midst of pain."[6]

***

My mental letter to Jeanie was growing a bit long, so in my heart I gave her a big hug and sent it off with a prayer. But God hadn't finished with *me* yet.

I recently received a disturbing letter from another friend. The pages were filled with tragic news of a husband who remarried the day after he divorced her, of a divorced daughter and grandson who moved in with her because they needed help, of her need to work at a menial job just to keep the roof above their heads, of rejection and sorrow and pain. Her concluding words, however, were edged with gold: "I can only live for eternity. There seems to be nothing left down here." How important—imperative—while suffering, to keep our eyes on our future place of residence: heaven.

Just Think

Of stepping on shore
    and finding it heaven!
Of taking hold of a hand,
    and finding it God's hand;
Of breathing new air
    and finding it celestial air;

> Of feeling invigorated,
>   and finding it immortality;
> Of passing from storm and tempest
>   to an unbroken calm;
> Of waking up—
>   and finding it Home.

In order to experience spiritual victory, we must recognize that these present circumstances are not a mistake someone has made but a part of God's unique plan fashioned just for us.

If we really know and believe that whatever we are experiencing is from God and that it comes to us with *love* . . . if our eyes are truly on eternity . . . if we are convinced that suffering is making us more like our Savior . . . if we are sure that His strength will enable us to endure— these very attitudes will help us as we "suffer according to God's will." But perhaps the thing that will encourage us above all others is to look at the *results* of doing God's will.

We are told in Scripture, "Do not throw away your confidence; it will be richly rewarded. You need to persevere so that when you have done the will of God, you will receive what he has promised" (Hebrews 10:35-36).

What has God promised? What *hasn't* He promised? He has promised us eternity, abundant life here and now, riches that will never be exhausted, peace, and joy. He is the great I AM . . . and we fill in the blank. I hang on to that promise.

Eternity—Eternity will be our inheritance as we do His will. "The world and its desires pass away, but the man who does the will of God lives forever" (1 John 2:17).

Answered prayer—When we do and desire the will of God, we can be assured that our prayers will be answered. "This is the assurance we have in approaching God: that

if we ask anything according to his will, he hears us"
(1 John 5:14). How can we know that we are praying according to His will? Praying Scripture is one way. And what
joy to know that the Holy Spirit always prays according to
God's will and that this Spirit dwells in us! (Romans 8:27).
So if we are sensitive to the Spirit, we are assured that
we are praying in God's will and that God will hear
and answer.

Wisdom and discernment—And then there are the
qualities of wisdom and discernment—qualities I long for.
If we obey God's will, we will know what comes from God
and what may be man's inventions. Jesus Himself said,
"My teaching is not my own. It comes from him who sent
me. If any one chooses to do God's will, he will find out
whether my teaching comes from God or whether I speak
on my own. He who speaks on his own does so to gain
honor for himself, but he who works for the honor of
the one who sent him is a man of truth; there is nothing
false about him" (John 7:16-18).

Maturity—Maturity is another giant result of doing
God's will. Paul told the Colossians, "Epaphras . . . is always
wrestling in prayer for you, that you may stand firm in all the
will of God, mature and fully assured" (Colossians 4:12).

Standing firm in doing what is right will make us grow
up and mature in every area of life. Swimming against
the current in the river of life makes for strong muscles.
But swimming upstream isn't easy—an understatement of
the first magnitude. Temptations run rampant through the
texture of our days. But maturity means holiness and a
life lived worthy of the Lord (Colossians 1:9-12, Hebrews
10:10). As mature saints, we are living sacrifices, holy
and pleasing to God, transformed and able to know that
His will is good, pleasing, and perfect (Romans 12:1-2
Ephesians 6:6).

I almost came out of my seat when I read Romans 5:2-5 in *The Living Bible*.

> Because of our faith, he has brought us into this place of highest privilege where we now stand, and we confidently and joyfully look forward to actually becoming all that God has had in mind for us to be.
>
> We can rejoice, too, when we run into problems and trials for we know that they are good for us—they help us learn to be patient. And patience develops strength of character in us and helps us trust God more each time we use it until finally our hope and faith are strong and steady. Then, when that happens, we are able to hold our heads high no matter what happens and know that all is well, for we know how dearly God loves us, and we feel this warm love everywhere within us because God has given us the Holy Spirit to fill our hearts with his love.

Does you heart leap when you read those words? Do you—do I—pray that God will teach us His will and that we will yearn to do it with *all* our hearts? David prayed, "I desire to do your will, O my God; your law is within my heart" (Psalm 40:8).

One attitude is mandatory: a wholeheartedness that holds nothing back, "doing the will of God from your heart. Serve wholeheartedly, as if you were serving the Lord, not men" (Ephesians 6:6-7).

Oswald Chambers said, "I have no business in God's service if I have any personal reserve; I am to be broken bread and poured-out wine in His hands."[7]

"God is voting for us all the time. The devil is voting against us all the time. The way we vote carries the election."[8] A wise observation from Corrie ten Boom.

Suffering is a major part of God's will for Christians. When we are full of the knowledge of God's will, we will understand this fact and open our arms wide to accept it. We will "welcome trials as friends." As we do, we will grow in maturity, in righteousness, in the ability to keep our mind focused on eternity.

My friend Jeanie isn't wasting her sorrows.

Are *you?*

NOTES: 1. "Coping with Crises," *Reader's Digest*, October 1980, page 65.
2. *Bright Legacy*, page 115.
3. Grant C. Tullar, *Faith, Prayer and Tract League* (Grand Rapids: Silent Evangelist), number 53.
4. Corrie ten Boom, *Each New Day* (Minneapolis: Worldwide Publications, 1978), January 7.
5. Gladys Hunt, *Don't Be Afraid to Die* (Grand Rapids: Zondervan), page 64.
6. Myers, *Discovering God's Will*, page 37.
7. Oswald Chambers, *Disciples Indeed* (Ft. Washington, PA: Christian Literature Crusade Publishing, 1960).
8. Corrie ten Boom, *Each New Day*, January 8.

APPLICATION BIBLE STUDY

1. Read slowly Hebrews 10:35-36 and then write these verses out in your own words. List several of God's promises in Scripture that have been important to you.

2. Name as many of the results of being filled with the knowledge of God's will as you can, including those discussed in this chapter. Which two of these results mean most to you? Explain.

3. Read Romans 12:1-2 in two versions. Spend five minutes praying about how this passage relates to your life.

4. On page 115, Romans 5:2-5 is quoted from *The Living Bible.* Read this passage aloud and slowly. Are you able to hold your head high "no matter what happens and know that all is well"? If not, what are you lacking from the previous verses in this passage? What do you think God would have you do about it?

5. Memorize Hebrews 10:36.

12
Filled with the Fruit of Righteousness

T HE DOORBELL RANG. Although a bit impatient with the interruption in my day, I hurried to answer. Immediately my impatience evaporated when I saw Jean, a new member of our Bible study, standing there. She said, "You looked tired at Bible study Tuesday. I thought I'd just bring this by to you." She handed me a freshly baked, still warm apple pie.

The prayer of Paul in Philippians 1:9-11 came to my mind: "This is my prayer: that your love may abound more and more in knowledge and depth of insight, so that you may be able to discern what is best and may be pure and blameless until the day of Christ, *filled* with the fruit of

117

righteousness that comes through Jesus Christ—to the glory and praise of God."

I thought, "Jean doesn't know it, but to me she is filled with the fruit of righteousness that comes through Jesus." Her visit—and that pie—made my day.

I define a friend as one who demonstrates God's goodness and righteousness to me.

In a church bulletin appeared this anecdote:

> Our rider lawn mower had broken down and I had been working fruitlessly for two hours trying to get it back together.
>
> Suddenly, my new neighbor appeared with a handful of tools. "Can I give you a hand?" he asked. In twenty minutes he had the mower functioning beautifully.
>
> "Thanks a million," I told him. "Say, what do you make with such a fine kit of tools?"
>
> "Mostly friends," he smiled.
>
> "I'm available any time."

Being a true friend is part of being filled with the fruit of righteousness. But it is only a part.

To be *righteous* is to act in a just or fair manner. First John 3:7 focuses in on the essence of the matter: "He who does what is right is righteous, just as he [Christ] is righteous." Being righteous means *acting like a Christian.*

The story is told of Alexander the Great, who was the sole judge of his army. At his command, heads were lopped off and punishment of all kinds doled out. A young soldier was brought before him one day who had gone to sleep while on duty. Alexander asked him what his name was.

"A-a-a-alexander, sir," the young soldier stammered.

"*What* did you say your name was?" the commander shouted.

"A-a-a-alexander, sir," the man repeated, terrified.

Alexander the Great got up from his seat, came down

and grabbed the soldier by his coat. Their faces inches apart, the commander thundered, "Soldier, either change your behavior or change your *name!*"

We as Christ-ones—named after the Lord Jesus Christ—may need to think long and hard about that. Sometimes, if I were sitting in the judgment seat of God, I know I'd thunder to me, "'Christian,' either change your behavior or change your *name.*" (I'm glad God is more patient with me than I would be!)

Righteousness—doing what is right—leads to holiness. We are told to give our bodies "in slavery to righteousness leading to holiness" (Romans 6:19). Righteousness is doing, holiness is being. Righteousness is something you do, holiness is something you become.

Righteousness is the result of God's light in us, "for the fruit of the light consists in all goodness, righteousness and truth" (Ephesians 5:9).

The results of righteousness are staggering. The person who is righteous will never be shaken. "He whose walk is blameless and who does what is righteous, who speaks the truth from his heart and has no slander on his tongue, who does his neighbor no wrong . . . will never be shaken" (Psalm 15:2-5).

That is quite something, isn't it? I fall so short in this venture, for I'm shaken—or close to being shaken—often.

The other day I turned right on a red light—it's legal in Colorado—without realizing how fast the oncoming traffic was going, especially one very large Chevrolet van. Obviously the driver was upset that I'd pulled into his path. At 50 mph (in a 40 mph zone), he almost hit the rear of my small car before swerving into the other lane, missing me by a hair's breadth. I could almost hear him saying, "That'll teach *her!*"

Following the silver and black van for several blocks,

I got a mental picture of the owner. The large amount of chrome shined to mirror-image brightness (perfectionist) and the fully-equipped four-wheel drive vehicle with chains and CB antennae (outdoorsman) told me something. But the mudguards were what made me sure I wouldn't want to meet that man. They pictured a western comic-strip character brandishing two six-guns pointed toward me, with large letters saying, "BACK OFF."

I was close to being shaken that day—not just because of my lack of "doing what was right" (turning too soon into traffic), but because of the van driver's lack of doing right as well.

At times, I do right—but with a wrong attitude.

Lynn was five and knew better! Jack was away, and Lynn and I were in church, sitting toward the front. The sermon had just begun.

The president of the organization where Jack worked sat in the pew ahead of us, his daughter electing to sit beside Lynn. Lynn began to talk in an animated way with Jean—out loud.

Annoyed, I glanced at her and said, "Shhhhh."

She continued talking.

"Lynn, be quiet," I commanded in a stern whisper.

It was as though I hadn't spoken.

Angrily, I said, "Lynn, if you don't stop, I'm going to take you outside and spank you."

I might just as well have been a soft breeze.

Embarrassed, frustrated, mad, I now found myself in the awful position of having to do what I'd threatened. I took my daughter firmly by the hand and we left our seats.

An aisle was never so long. In the forever walk up the church, Lynn shrieked steadily, "No, Mommy, No, Mommy, *NO!*"

Outside, I carried out the promised spanking firmly

on her backside. As I sat in the car waiting for her sobs to cease, my own fury abated. It was then that I heard the inner voice: "Who, then, will spank *you* for being so angry?"

I could not respond.

I was not amiss in removing Lynn from church, nor unjust for disciplining her for her disobedience. But I was wrong to punish her in anger.

How glad I am that God never punishes His children out of anger, but only out of His great heart of love. His thought is not to express His disfavor, but to teach us to be better people.

I may have done right . . . but I did it with a wrong attitude, negating any possible fruit of righteousness.

It was then that I decided to take a good, hard look at the characteristics of a righteous person. I found that a righteous person will be happy and thankful (Psalms 106:3, 118:19). He will attain real life (Proverbs 11:19) and will be loved in a special way by God (Proverbs 15:9).

Aren't you glad that God so patiently unravels when we tangle our lives so often by wrong attitudes and actions?

> With thoughtless and
>   Impatient hands,
>   We tangle up
>   The plans
> The Lord hath wrought.
>
> And when we cry,
>   In pain, He saith,
>   "Be quiet, dear,
> While I untie the knot."[1]

Our need is to act rightly with perseverance and steadfastness, for righteousness becomes an armor against Satan, guarding us from his attacks. It gives us a weapon to use against him (Proverbs 13:6, 2 Corinthians 6:7).

Have you ever considered how righteousness guards us?

Some blackmailers once sent Spurgeon a letter stating that if he did not place a certain amount of money in a certain place at a certain time, they would publish some things in the newspapers that would defame him and ruin his public ministry. He left at that designated place a letter in reply: "You and your like are requested to publish all you know about me across the heavens."[2] He knew that his life was blameless in the eyes of men, thus they could not touch his character.

Righteousness, like truth, guards our lives against the attacks of Satan. The source of our righteousness is Christ alone. We are credited with His righteousness when we accept Him into our lives (Romans 4:6-8). "For if, by the trespass of the one man, death reigned through that one man, how much more will those who receive God's abundant provision of grace and of the gift of righteousness reign in life through the one man, Jesus Christ" (Romans 5:17).

God not only gives us Christ's righteousness, but as He lives in us, He *is* our righteousness. "God made him who had no sin to be sin for us, so that in him we might become the righteousness of God" (2 Corinthians 5:21).

If we look through a piece of red glass, everything is red; through blue glass, everything is blue, and so on. When we believe in Jesus Christ as our Savior, God looks at us through the Lord Jesus Christ. He sees us in all the white holiness of His Son. Our sins are imputed to the account of Christ and His righteousness to our account.

Positionally, then, in the eyes of God we *are* righteous, declared so by God Himself because Christ lives in us. But practically—in this life, going on right now, this minute—

THE FRUIT OF RIGHTEOUSNESS

we are *becomers*. God's purpose is for us to become in this life what He has already declared us to be—righteous. He wants us to do what is right. And that's where the work comes in, doesn't it?

And my old question surfaces once again. How?
God spells it out.

1. *We should hunger for righteousness.* Jesus declared, "Blessed are those who hunger and thirst for righteousness, for they will be *filled*" (Matthew 5:6). There it is again—not only righteousness, but being *filled*! If we find ourselves not hungering for righteousness, then we need to pray for that hunger. How often in the last month have you asked God to give you an overwhelming desire to be righteous? Begin to pray for it consistently, and then watch what happens.

2. *We should offer ourselves to God,* in total surrender of everything we are and have. "Do not offer the parts of your body to sin, as instruments of wickedness, but rather offer yourselves to God, as those who have been brought from death to life; and offer the parts of your body to him as instruments of righteousness" (Romans 6:13). This surrender should be a part of our daily devotional time. As I'm writing this, I realize I've become very sloppy and sporadic about my prayer life, so I've just spent a few minutes asking God to help me be more consistent.

3. *We should obey God's commandments.* "Don't you know that when you offer yourselves to someone to obey him as slaves, you are slaves to the one whom you obey—whether you are slaves to sin, which leads to death, or to obedience, which leads to righteousness?" (Romans 6:16; see also John 15:2-8).

4. *We should depend on His power.* "He who supplies seed to the sower and bread for food will also supply and increase your store of seed and will enlarge the harvest of *your righteousness*" (2 Corinthians 9:10).

5. *We should die to ourselves and put on a new self* (Ephesians 4:24, John 12:24). This one isn't easy! (Are any of them?) It is first of all a matter of our wills. Dying to self means dying to *pride*. And pride is so insidious! Just when I think I've got a handle on it, something else pops up.

There used to be a TV program about a person who could become invisible and visible at will. He had the ability to make himself either seen or unseen in order to carry out his adventures.

There are times when I feel as if I've unintentionally pressed a wrong button, suddenly rendering me invisible— only I can't find the right switch, words, or formula to make me reappear.

To certain people, I'm simply not there. It's not that I'm either heard or not heard, accepted or rejected, friend or foe, appreciated or not appreciated. I'm just *nothing*. A blank. A phantom. A nonentity.

I've gone through all kinds of emotions about this sometimes state. Pity. Questions. (Why don't they notice me? Don't they like me? What have I done?) Feelings of inadequacy. Hurt. Anger. (I'm not going to ask her to lunch anymore until she calls *me*!)

I'm beginning to realize that I do have a problem. But my problem isn't being invisible. It lies in the reason I so desperately want to *be* visible to people. My problem is in myself.

I want people to notice me, affirm me, be aware of my abilities. And I ought to call that by name. It is *pride*.

King David was never invisible, but countless times he suffered rejection and betrayal. He certainly did a lot of things wrong, but one thing he did *right*. He never retaliated! David's constant forgiveness and tenderheartedness toward Absalom, Shimei, and Sheba constantly amaze me. Because David learned humility when he saw the fickleness of people, he developed a concern for pleasing *God alone.*

But I want to be noticed. I want Jack to be noticed. I want to be affirmed and appreciated.

I go about this in subtle and not-so-subtle ways. I may make statements like, "I don't think I did that very well," hoping that someone will say, "Oh, that was great." I phrase things—sometimes subconsciously, but not always—in a way that pleads for sympathy or recognition.

But God has me on a growing edge along the fine line of teaching me about pride and humility. This morning He reminded me that "Christ *made Himself* of no reputation." My NIV says, "He made himself *nothing*" (Philippians 2:7). And *He* is to be my example!

How do I make myself nothing? By giving God and others permission to make me invisible. By building up others, not only out loud but also in my own mind. By rejoicing when others are visible and I'm not. By not place-dropping, name-dropping, event-dropping. By knowing that I'm nothing—yet knowing that I'm everything because He lives in me and that I am valuable to Him. By being one hundred percent concerned with what God thinks of me and unconcerned about what people think. By saying in my heart, "Go ahead, world. Wipe your feet on me!" Wow! That's even hard to write, let alone to feel. I want to get to the place where the important issue is not whether or not the world does wipe its feet on me, but whether my heart's response to *whatever* God allows in my life is "Hallelujah!"

I'm not there yet. I'm still a becomer. But to me, this is a part of "dying to self." A.W. Tozer, in *The Pursuit of God*, put it this way:

> The meek man is not a human mouse afflicted with a sense of his own inferiority. Rather he may be in his moral

life as bold as a lion and as strong as Samson; but he has stopped being fooled about himself.

He has accepted God's estimate of his own life. He knows he is as weak and helpless as God has declared him to be, but paradoxically, he knows at the same time that he is in the sight of God of more importance than angels. In himself, nothing; in God, everything. That is his motto.

He knows well that the world will never see him as God sees him and he has stopped caring. He rests perfectly content to allow God to place His own values. He will be patient to wait for the day when everything will get its own price tag and real worth will come into its own. Then the righteous shall shine forth in the Kingdom of their Father.[2]

6. *We should pray for righteousness and pray for others that they will become righteous.* "Open for me the gates of righteousness; I will enter and give thanks to the Lord" (Psalm 118:19). Paul prayed that the Philippian people would be "filled with the fruit of righteousness" (Philippians 1:11).

7. *Lastly, we should pursue righteousness—go for it, work at it.* "But you, man of God, flee from all this, and pursue righteousness, godliness, faith, love, endurance and gentleness" (1 Timothy 6:11).

Did you ever want to kick yourself? Sometimes I get discouraged with myself because, with all God has given me, I should be a giant in the faith instead of a pygmy.

Take a sanguine/phlegmatic female with godly parents;
Add Bible-teaching churches, inspiring Christian camps;
Mix in a Christian college education;
Combine with a loving, loyal husband who is single-
    minded in following God;
Add a child who delights the heart;

Stir it with years of joys and sorrows, moments of
      pain and heartache, victories and defeats;
Then heap in an immeasurable amount of God's grace.

The result of these ingredients should arrive from God's refining oven in the form of a saint like Amy Carmichael or Mother Teresa. Instead, they come out . . . me.

On the other hand—

Take a woman born into slavery;
Add a misguided mistress;
Mix in a situation requiring her to have relations
      with her mistress's husband and to bear his child;
Stir it with jealousy, disappointment, insecurity.

The result should be a bitter heathen. Instead comes out the mother of the Arab nations—Hagar—who listened to God and submitted to her stern mistress Sarah, becoming a significant part of the will of God for the future of the world (see Genesis 16).

I am convinced that I am not going to be judged for my works in a straight comparison to the works of others. (Fortunately we Christ-ones will *never* be judged for our sins—they have forever been buried with Christ—but we *will* be judged by our works.)

Filtered into the data-processing of God's great computer, I think will be all the advantages, blessings, heritage, prayers, and temperaments that each of us have had ladled out to us in the course of life. When the printout appears, it will be a reading of what I *should* or *could* have been or done in proportion to what was given to me. "From everyone who has been given much, much will be demanded; and from the one who has been entrusted with much, much more will be asked (Luke 12:48).

Of course, comparison is fruitless in any case, so it is

senseless for me to dwell on what I should or could be, given the various components of my life. My focus must be on obeying God and doing right *this day*. Comparison is, either negatively or positively, a distraction from this sense of immediacy.

God wants our lives to be a harvest of righteousness and peace. He wants each of us to be *filled* with righteousness. So do we.

Let's go for it!

NOTES: 1. V. Raymond Edman, *The Disciplines of Life* (Eugene, OR: Harvest House Publishers), page 43.
   2. A.W. Tozer, *The Pursuit of God* (Harrisburg: Christian Publications, 1948), page 113.

APPLICATION BIBLE STUDY

1. Read carefully Philippians 1:9-11 and then write it out in your own words. Define the word "righteousness," then define the "fruit of righteousness."

2. Explain in your own words how we achieve righteousness according to these verses:
   (a) Matthew 5:6
   (b) Romans 6:13-16
   (c) 2 Corinthians 9:10
   (d) Ephesians 4:24
   (e) 1 Timothy 6:11
   (f) Hebrews 12:11
   (g) James 3:18

3. Pray for God to lay on your heart one "righteous" thing to do each day this week. Write each down, and do it.

4. From these verses, what are some results of righteousness and its fruit?
   (a) Psalm 15:2-3
   (b) Proverbs 11:19
   (c) Proverbs 15:9

(d) Proverbs 21:21
(e) Isaiah 32:17
(f) Romans 6:19
(g) Ephesians 6:14
(h) Philippians 1:11

13
Filled with Light,
Overflowing with Hope

S HE SAT TWO aisles and one booth away from where I stood, unnoticed by most of the ebb and flow of the large booksellers convention. She read quietly, this diminutive woman with wisdom-wrinkles lining her face, her turbaned hair coiled in a round bun. Occasionally, a person stopped at her booth, at which point warmth reached out to them, hands passed out the books and other literature lining the table before her. I had walked by her cubicle a few times, scarcely noting the modest display, which was dwarfed by the gargantuan booths surrounding hers.

And then a passerby said, "Did you know that Sabina Wurmbrand is here?"

I said, "Sabina Wurmbrand? The wife of Richard who wrote *Tortured for Christ*?"

"Yes," he replied, and nodded toward the unassuming woman a few yards away.

Awed, I turned. No hoopla. No signs announcing who she was or what her life had entailed. No publicity. No "personality booth" autographing time, although she is an author in her own right and the wife of a man who at that very moment was meeting with a group of U.S. senators. No line to stand in as I went to meet her. Just a smile that glowed with the light of Christ, radiating warmth to a fellow-believer and sister in the Lord.

That week I had been privileged to meet senators, outstanding speakers, and celebrities at the convention. But the highlight for me was shaking hands with a woman who had suffered imprisonment in a Communist country, separation from her family, torture, poverty, and unbelievable atrocities for the cause of Christ—a woman who, despite and because of all those trials of her faith, remained a humble, untouted, unpublicized *saint of God*.

In the brief moments that we spoke, Sabina exemplified some other qualities that we as Christians are to be filled with, and one in particular with which we are to overflow.

She was filled with Christ's light, filled with understanding, and *overflowing* with hope.

Light.

The word *light* means "radiance, illumination, brightness, understanding, insight."[1]

In the Sermon on the Mount, the Lord Jesus pulled no punches, clouded no issues. He said clearly, "The eye is the lamp of the body. If your eyes are good, your whole body will be full of light" (Matthew 6:22).

God doesn't want me to have just a little bit of light. He wants me to be *filled* with light. And He even tells me how. "Watch out that the sunshine isn't blotted out. If you are filled with light within, with no dark corners, then your face will be radiant too, as though a floodlight is beamed upon you" (Luke 11:35-36, *The Living Bible*).

No humanly natural light resides in me. All was dark until the light of Christ came into my life. He is light and the only source of it. "The Lord is my light and my salvation—whom shall I fear? The Lord is the stronghold of my life—of whom shall I be afraid?" (Psalm 27:1). Christ declared for the world to hear, "I am the light of the world. Whoever follows me will never walk in darkness, but will have the light of life" (John 8:12).

Mine is reflected light. But that reflected light—"as though a floodlight is beamed upon you"—is to be radiant. Undimmed. Brilliant.

Elizabeth Rooney writes, "The sun has come over the horizon and the eastern side of every leaf and branch and tree trunk is glistening with gold. I feel like that. I'm always the same twig, but to the extent that I allow myself to be suffused with God as the trees are with sunlight I am transformed, golden and glistening. I don't have to do anything except stay in the same place and be still and let him come."[2]

Christ lives within anyone who has accepted Him as Savior. My responsibility, now that I am alive, is to shine—to keep the windows of my soul free from dirt and grime so that His light can shine through clearly.

The symbolism is unlimited. Light dispels darkness. Light guides our way. Light makes things grow. Light warms us, cheers us. The list goes on.

But perhaps one of the most meaningful is that light brings illumination and understanding.

Often this light helps me to understand the purpose of God's timing of events, the working of God within people. But there is an even broader, more comprehensive sense of understanding—an understanding we are to be *full of*. Paul writes in Colossians 2:2-3, "My purpose is that they may be encouraged in heart and united in love, so that they may have the full riches of complete understanding, in order that they may know the mystery of God, namely, Christ, in whom are hidden all the treasures of wisdom and knowledge."

"Full riches of complete understanding." Quite an order, isn't it?

The phone rang early one Friday, and I left the warmth of my bed to stumble my way to answer. A friend, her voice breaking, detailed the tragic event.

The previous Sunday, the husband of a mutual friend had been carrying an oak chest to the basement. His wife had begged him to wait for their son to help, but he was a tall, strong man in his forties who assured her he could handle it. When she heard the terrible crash and saw him lying there, she ran to phone the paramedics. He had fallen, hitting his head, landing with the chest on top of him. Blood clots on the brain made surgery necessary, and now, five days later, he was dead.

"I don't understand, Lord," I said. "Mary Lou loves you so much. She is serving you with all her heart. I just don't understand."

I had really expected the phone call early that morning to be from Jack, who had flown to California to be with his mother after his father had suffered a heart attack following pacemaker surgery. On top of extensive damage to the heart, his hiccups had returned. For three years, he had had the convulsive type of hiccups that resist every medication and procedure—a couple weeks with them, a few days without. After three years and a multitude of prayers, they had stopped. But now they had returned, weakening the already worn-out heart of a beloved husband and father.

"Lord, You healed Dad of the hiccups before. Why allow them to return when Dad is so weak? If You want to take him Home to be with You, can't You do it in a more gentle way? I just don't understand."

He whispered to my heart, "You don't have to understand. Only trust."

I argued, "But Lord, You said in Colossians that I should have the full riches of complete understanding."

He answered, "Dear child, you didn't read the whole verse."

I read on then: ". . . may have the full riches of complete understanding, in order that they may know the mystery of God, namely, Christ, in whom are hidden all the treasures of wisdom and knowledge. I tell you this so that no one may deceive you by fine-sounding arguments"—or wrong interpretation!

I sighed and prayed, "Forgive me, Lord. You didn't say that I'd understand everything about events, or people, or pain. You said that I'd be filled with knowledge about You, and, really, that's all I need, isn't it?"

He answered, "*Now* you understand."

***

Sabina Wurmbrand was not only filled with light and understanding: she was also *overflowing with hope*.

I cry inside to see the lack of hope in the world around us. But can you and I truly say of our lives that we are "overflowing with hope"?

On May 7, 1983 I wrote these words:

I sit in my favorite brown Naugahyde chair, my feet, clad in tennis shoes from my morning walk, on the matching ottoman. The house is quiet. Only the soft, familiar sounds of the schoolhouse clock ticking above the fireplace and the occasional clicking on of the furnace and refrigerator interrupt the stillness.

It is Saturday morning. Generally when we are in town, Saturday is a "have-breakfast-at-Denny's day" with Jack, then errands, shopping, and a relaxed afternoon watching a golf match on TV. Today Jack is with his mother in California, helping her with his critically ill dad.

I decide the house is too quiet and wonder what I'd do as a widow.

My thoughts go back to the verse I've been contemplating recently: "May the God of hope fill you with all joy and peace as you trust in him, so that you may overflow with hope by the power of the Holy Spirit" (Romans 15:13). I wonder what this really means. Is this a sometimes thing or should it be always present in our lives? What makes us overflow with hope? Hope of what? Am I overflowing with hope right now on this lonely, quiet day?

Suddenly my heart answers, *Yes!* I am overflowing with hope. Not a "wish-for-pie-in-the-sky" type of hope, but a hope that is born of sureness, expectancy, and life. An "I-know-so" hope.

My hope overflows because I know that if Dad dies, it is only his worn-out body that will be laid in a grave. His spirit will soar and sing so that he will be more vitally *alive* than he's ever been before. He'll laugh and converse and behold wonders he's never even imagined.

I'm overflowing with that kind of hope.

Job described the magnificence of the stars, moon, clouds, and the sea as merely the outer *fringe* of God's works (Job 26:14). I overflow with hope—a sure hope—that one day I will see the whole garment in all its splendor and glory.

I think of Joye, of Dad, of Mom, of both grandfathers

and grandmothers, and of the many dear friends who reside now in heaven. My heart overflows with hope that I will join them one day.

I think of Jesus—the love of Christ, my Lord. My hope overflows knowing that I will see Him face to face and come into the inheritance He has reserved for me in a place without pain, sorrow, tears, or frustrations.

There will be perfect understanding then. I won't wonder anymore why babies die, why nations starve, why people suffer. I will understand.

I *am* overflowing with hope—even on this quiet, lonely, rather sad day. My Redeemer lives! And because He lives, I too shall live. He himself is Hope. "Christ in you, the hope of glory" (Colosssians 1:27).

***

I love Benjamin De Casseres's definition of hope: "Hope is the gay, skylarking pajamas we wear over yesterday's bruises."[3] I love it—but it is *so much more than that.*

The opposite of hope is despair. Despair and hope cannot coexist. Our hope is to be in God, in the resurrection of the dead, in the wonderful promises of our Lord. We are to hope in God's glory, in righteousness, in God's calling, in eternal life, and in Christ's return.[4]

Rolling all these "hopes" together, shaking them down into one colossal heap, we would declare, "Base your happiness on your hope in Christ" (Romans 12:12, *Phillips*).

The characteristics of hope are incredibly vital to our spiritual life. Hope will not disappoint us; it is wrapped up in love; it is an anchor of the soul, sure and steadfast.[5]

We all want hope, both for the joy it produces and for the valuable traits it builds into our lives: joy, peace, boldness of speech and effective ministry, love, steadfastness, encouragement, diligence, and purity of life.[6]

Oh, we all want what hope produces. But some of us may not be willing to pay the price to obtain it. And there *is* a price.

When we possess hope, we have a responsibility—a great one—in two major areas. We have a responsibility to share this hope with others, to be ready to give an answer to everyone who wants to know the reason for the hope within us, in gentleness and reverence (1 Peter 3:15). Furthermore, we have a responsibility to purify ourselves. "Every one who has this hope fixed on Him purifies himself, just as He is pure" (1 John 3:3, NASB).

To meet these responsibilities, we have to first possess this hope in our Lord. And how do we nurture hope until it expands and grows and finally spills over to every part of our lives?

***

Four tender buds of hope must be cultivated.

We grow in hope through our *perseverance and encouragement from the Scriptures*. Does this sound like a broken record? Our total fulfillment is anchored in this truth. "For everything that was written in the past was written to teach us, so that through endurance and the encouragement of the Scriptures we might have hope" (Romans 15:4).

Reading Job (yes, *Job*) that afternoon when my heart was troubled over the death of my friend's husband and the illness of dear Dad, gave me true and deep *hope*. Often I am driven to the Scriptures in discouraging times. Never have I failed to find God's comfort, peace, and hope. This kind of hope may take more than a hurried, "Lord, help." It may take our patient dedication for an hour or two as we pour our hearts out to Him and then wait for Him to speak—to give to us what I call "a hundred-pound sack of His grace."

The second bud for us to nurture is *praying for hope*
Pray for hope and get others to pray for you. For it is *God*
who gives endurance, encouragement, joy, and peace so
that we may "overflow with hope by the power of the Holy
Spirit" (Romans 15:13).

The third bud of hope takes *work* in order to grow
(not that prayer and searching God's word don't). This
outcropping of hope comes through *diligence*. Diligence
in helping others, in "imitating" those who have gone before
us—the saints of old—and in keeping on keeping on. "God
is not unjust; he will not forget your work and the love
you have shown him as you have helped his people and
continue to help them. We want each of you to show this
same *diligence* to the very end, in order to make your
hope sure. We do not want you to become lazy, but to
imitate those who through faith and patience inherit what
has been promised" (Hebrews 6:10-12).

I was amazed to find out that the word "hope" is used
sixteen times in the book of Job. Talk about hanging on!

The fourth bud of hope is grown and pruned through
suffering. Read slowly and carefully Romans 5:1-5:

> Therefore, since we have been justified through faith, we
> have peace with God through our Lord Jesus Christ, through
> whom we have gained access by faith into this grace in
> which we now stand. And we rejoice in the hope of the
> glory of God. Not only so, but we also rejoice in our
> sufferings, because we know that suffering produces
> perseverance; perseverance, character; and character, hope.
> And hope does not disappoint us, because God has poured
> out his love into our hearts by the Holy Spirit, whom
> he has given us.

Suffering produces perseverance, perseverance produces
character, and character produces hope. Suffering, in a

succession of events, then, gives us a solid, far-reaching sense of hope.

It has always been thus.

A friend of mine wrote the following words explaining the logic in the importance of suffering:

> It has been helpful for me . . . to reflect on the life and ministry of our Lord and to remember . . . there was the *cross before the crown.* There has to be a battle before there can be a victory. The door to success swings on the hinges of opposition. Without fail, when we look at the saints of Scripture, we see that conflict precedes blessing.
>
> Joseph—Prison preceded prime minister.
>
> Moses—Forty years in the wilderness preceded his leading the nation of Israel.
>
> Joshua—War throughout Canaan preceded peace and prosperity.
>
> Job—Great physical and emotional conflict preceded unprecedented prosperity.
>
> And on . . . and on . . . and on.[7]

Look around you and see those people who have depth in their lives. They have suffered. And this suffering has produced character. And that inner strength of character has produced hope.

George Mueller, a great man of faith, said, "God delights to increase the faith of His children. We ought, instead of wanting no trials before victory, no exercise for patience, to be willing to take them from God's hand as a means. I say—and say it deliberately—trials, obstacles, difficulties, and sometimes defeats, are the very food of faith."

Filled with light and understanding. Overflowing with hope. The prize is more than worth the price.

Sabina, thanks for your example.

NOTES: 1. From *Reader's Digest Word Finder*.
2. *Bright Legacy*, page 112.
3. Benjamin De Casseres, from "Quotable Quotes," *Reader's Digest*, April 1983, page 59.
4. Acts 28:15, 1 Peter 1:31, Acts 26:6-7, Romans 8:23, 5:2, Galatians 5:5, Ephesians 1:18, Titus 1:2, 2:13.
5. Romans 5:5, 1 Corinthians 13:7, Hebrews 1:18-20.
6. 1 Peter 1:3, Romans 12:15, 2 Corinthians 3:12, Colossians 1:5, 1 Thessalonians 1:3, 5:11, Hebrews 6:11, 1 John 3:3.
7. Terry Taylor, "Dear Staff Letter," September 1982.

APPLICATION BIBLE STUDY

1. Read slowly Psalm 25, and list all the things the psalmist hopes for.

2. According to these verses, what is the content of our hope?
   (a) Acts 24:15
   (b) Romans 5:2
   (c) Romans 8:19-21
   (d) Romans 8:23
   (e) Colossians 1:27
   (f) Titus 1:2
   (g) 1 Peter 1:13

3. According to Romans 5:1-5 and 15:4,5,13, how do we obtain this hope?

4. What does hope produce in us according to the following verses?
   (a) Romans 12:12
   (b) 2 Corinthians 3:12
   (c) Colossians 1:4-5

5. Memorize a verse in this chapter that especially challenged or uplifted you.

14
Filled with Everything I Need

W E SING IT. We attest to it. We memorize it. We quote it as our favorite verse. We use it to comfort others. But we don't mean it. Not really.

We declare, "The Lord is my Shepherd, I shall not want" (Psalm 23:1). Mentally, most of us add a few lines to this verse. Oh, not out loud. But inwardly.

We think, "The Lord is my Shepherd. I shall not want . . . that is, if He gives me a loving husband. And health is a must, of course. I'm sure He wants me to have a caring family, too. And supportive friends. Then I need enough money for a lifestyle to which I'd like to become accustomed. And. . . ." The list goes on . . . and on . . . and on.

The truth is that we do want the Lord to be our Shepherd. But we are not content without the "pluses." *The Living Bible* gives an interesting rendering of this verse: "Because the Lord is my Shepherd, I have everything I need!" We add in our hearts, "but truthfully, I have several other wants to really make me happy."

Have you ever seriously thought about the statement David made to God in Psalm 145:16? "You open your hand and satisfy the desires of every living thing." Quite a comprehensive, inexhaustible promise, isn't it? This verse seems to be saying that whatever "the desires of every living thing" may be, God will satisfy them.

But *does* He? What about my friend whose alcoholic husband just left her? What about another dear one with a husband who hasn't supported her in years? What about the couple whose son is deteriorating rapidly with multiple sclerosis? They have desires for a happy marriage, for money enough to meet their needs, and for a strong and healthy son. But God doesn't seem to be filling *those* desires.

As I was contemplating and questioning this verse, a picture came to mind. (Friends, I don't really have visions— just an active, "sanctified" imagination.) A giant fist came down from heaven. Fascinated, I wondered about all the "good things" it would hold. My imagination ran wild. Slowly the hand opened. There was nothing in it! *Nothing but the hand itself.*

But then it struck me. This verse doesn't tell me that God is going to satisfy my want for *things*. Rather, it tells me that His character, His presence, *He Himself* is all I need. God is my sufficiency.

I looked at Jack sitting a few feet from me on the couch reading and I thought, "How I love you! After being married to you nearly thirty-four years, I love you more—much more—than the day we were married. You are such a *satis-*

fying husband." I smiled inwardly and added, "You are just what I need."

What was I really saying? That Jack has been able through the years to give me the material comforts of life? No. Certainly we haven't always had material comforts. That he has always met my emotional needs? No, not always, especially when he had to be away for long periods of time.

What I was really saying was that Jack, as a person, as a man, as a husband and companion, has been and is a person who is deeply satisfying to my heart. He is not perfect, nor am I, but God has fitted Jack to be the one in the world who brings to me great joy, comfort, and stability. His *character* satisfies me—not what he *gives* me, but who he *is*.

The character of God—who He is—will completely satisfy us if we open ourselves fully to Him. That doesn't mean that He doesn't want us to have the "pluses." He wants to delight us with bonuses of every scope and variety. But bonuses . . . pluses . . . extras are just *additional* things. They are not the things that are necessary in order for joy, peace, hope, understanding, and all the other ingredients with which we are to be filled.

If we are filled full with God Himself, then even joy, peace, and hope are by-products. They are the *result* of God in us.

So may our focus be on Him. May our dwelling be in Him. May our strength be through Him. May our joy, peace, hope, and understanding be by Him.

Until, at last, we are filled *to overflowing* with God Himself.